It's Time for School

It's Time for School

How to prepare yourself and your child for a
smooth transition that will make starting school a
positive experience

Cliff Schimmels

LIFEJOURNEY
BOOKS

David C. Cook Publishing Co.
Elgin, Illinois   Weston, Ontario

LifeJourney Books is an imprint of David C. Cook Publishing Co.
David C. Cook Publishing Co., Elgin, Illinois 60120
David C. Cook Publishing Co., Weston, Ontario

IT'S TIME FOR SCHOOL
(Also published as *The First Three Years of School*)
© 1989 Cliff Schimmels

Cover design by Russ Peterson
Book design by April Frost
Back cover photo by Ron Ericksen Photography

First printing, 1989
Printed in the United States of America
93 92 91 90 89 5 4 3 2 1

Schimmels, Cliff.
        It's Time for School
        1. Education, Primary—United States. 2. Child rearing—
            United   States. 3. Home and school—United
            States. I. Title
        LB 1507.S29 1989
        372.973—dc19
ISBN   1-55513-069-0
                                            89-763
                                             CIP

To Mary

Writing about child rearing is at best a presumptuous task, but I have a valuable source of help—a wise wife—one who is charming enough to encourage me, diplomatic enough to allow me to make some mistakes with her children, and unselfish enough to let me participate in some of the success and claim some of the ideas.

It seems rather paradoxical that I dedicate this book to her. Not only did she type it, proofread it, and supervise the writing, but she lived through and demonstrated the suggestions not once but three times.

In humble ways, I express my gratitude for all of this, and so much more.

CONTENTS

INTRODUCTION: OFF TO A GOOD START

The First Day of School

H e had become such a part of me. I had not really intended for it to happen that way, but it did. I had seen those overindulgent mothers before, and had promised myself that I would never become one. Nevertheless, he grew into a part of me, and I like to think that I grew into a part of him. Even when he was little, I enjoyed watching his personality form. I entertained myself for hours just by studying his facial expressions—the way he fixed his mouth when he was determined, the way he looked into space when he was frustrated, the way his eyes glistened when he was delighted. I appreciated his inquisitiveness, his creativity, his sweetness.

Somehow he always knew just what I needed. He knew when I was pensive and needed silence. He knew when I was lonely and needed his affection or to show my affection. He knew when I was jolly and needed his antics to amuse me. We were quite a pair, mother and son—carrying each other through each day and making it all worthwhile.

I knew that inevitable day would come and, on the outside, I looked forward to it. My husband and I had talked about it for months. This was a highlight, a benchmark, one of life's major milestones. But when *that big, yellow bus finally rolled up outside our yard and honked that blasted horn, I realized I wasn't prepared for all the emotions I was going to feel for the next twelve or thirteen years.*

For one thing, the bus looked so huge and impersonal. When he climbed up those steps with his tiny legs filled with purpose and disappeared into the bowels of that bus, I felt that I would never see him again—at least never as he was before.

Now I had to trust him to people I didn't even know. Sure, they all came with the best of credentials; but how long would it take them to learn to read the mouth and the eyes and the gaze? How long would it take them to realize that he could respond to their moods and help them through their day? Or would he lose that and become callous to other people's needs? And if he lost that, what else would he lose over the next decade?

I sat down and cried. A part of me died that day when I sent my son to that unknown, alien world called school. Now I fight feelings of jealousy and fear and distrust. I really want to be honest with the schools. I want to give them their chance and their credit, but I want those people to understand that I have entrusted them with a precious part of myself.

Since you are reading this book, you have probably already experienced some of the happiness and frustrations this young mother describes—the hollowness of that first day, the helplessness that comes when you realize your child will spend six hours a day, 180 days a year in that other world, in the care of people you may never meet, in a situation over which you have very little control. It is frightening—at least for anyone who deserves the title of parent.

I don't propose to alleviate all your fears, and I am not going to be dishonest about the power of the school in your child's formation. But I don't think the school world has to be all that foreign. Schools and school people aren't really as mysterious as they may seem. In fact, some are nice folks once you get to know them.

A Crucial Three Years

Why do parents begin to panic as their child gets ready to enter first grade? It's what you've been waiting for, isn't it? He's out of diapers; he can feed himself; he can carry on a conversation. It's time for him to wander a little farther out of the nest into that unknown world beyond. And you—you can breathe a bit, fix your nails, wash the car, take a walk alone.

But it's not an easy transition. One moment you glance at your child, and he looks so grown up—so independent, so ready to face nearly anything. The next minute you look back to see if your first appraisal was accurate, and you see a fragile infant full of innocence and emotions, just waiting for some outsider to chip away at all that you have grown to love in him. What's going to happen to him in that alien world called school?

During the first three years in school, your child will encounter more new things than he will during any other three-year period of his life.

First grade is a time of beginnings. Among the new experiences he'll encounter is that awesome experience of learning to unravel the mysteries of the universe through the printed word: he will learn to read. The thrill of newness carries a particular challenge to the learner and to the family who shares that world with him.

Second grade is a time of mastery. Your child has learned to read, to count, to write, to sit still; he has learned to learn. During second grade, he will have to grow with his newfound skills. He will have to master them. This time the thrill will not be in the newness, but in the freedom that comes from being able to do things on his own.

Third grade is a time of transition. Your child has learned and mastered new skills. Now, he must perfect those skills so that he can say good-bye to a child's world and begin to enter a world of independence and increased responsibility. When he learned to put words on paper in first grade, he was printing. That's child's writing. In third grade he will put aside that child's writing and write like an adult in cursive. In fact, writing serves as a symbol of the whole third-grade experience. Here the thrill is in the anticipation. The child can see a bigger world of independence ahead.

Although each of the three years is a different experience, the package constitutes a crucial age. During these years, your child will establish a base of brand-new skills and attitudes that will serve him the rest of his life. If any one of these years doesn't go right, he will probably have some extra work in the future to compensate. Thus it is imperative for all of us, parents and teachers, to cooperate in helping him get that base right. It is this imperative that gives this book its purpose.

Mom and Dad: Still #1

During the next three years, your child will need intelligent parents and a supportive family more than at any other time in his life, except when he was very young and totally dependent. It is very important to understand your child during this time, to understand what he is going through at school so you can complement and supplement all of his outside activities and bring them together to form a well-adjusted child.

That is the purpose of this book—to help you gain some understanding about what is happening to your child in that strange world of school, so you can encourage him, support him, and fill in the gaps the outside agencies miss. Remember, the home is still the most significant, most influential child-rearing and educating institution in this country.

Regardless of where you decide to send your child to school, regardless of how much money you spend on his education, regardless of how good or bad his teachers are, you are still the most significant influence in his development. If he is going to learn to read, count, add, multiply, tie his shoes, tell time, find his way home, drive, write poetry, play baseball, love, care, or worship, you are going to have to teach him.

Oh, you can expect a little help from some other places such as school or church. But you may not get it; and at best, it is only help. If your child is to become educated, you must assume the responsibility. As parents, your job is to help your child get through those first three years of school with a solid enough base in learning skills, self-identity, and fear of God that he can grow toward becoming what God has created him to be.

Homework Assignments for Parents

1. To what extent have you been involved in your child's education so far?

2. Upon starting school, did that amount of involvement increase, decrease, or remain about the same? Why?

3. In what ways can you begin to work in conjunction with the school system to continue to teach your child?

Looking Forward to a New Experience

Although some children seem to be excited about school before they leave the crib, I suspect most have some apprehensive moments as the time draws closer, even those who don't admit it. You can help your child handle those apprehensions by remembering to be positive about school as often as you can; but that may be tougher advice than it sounds.

It's easy to be negative about school without really meaning to. At least, it's easy for our children to interpret what we say as negative. When you and your friends sit around and reminisce about the pranks you pulled and the times you got into trouble with teachers for such major crimes as chewing gum or talking out of turn, your poor preschooler is listening and developing a bagful of doubts about the whole process.

Also, it is often quite easy to develop the habit of threatening a preschooler with the prospect of school:

"Sit still while I read to you. When you start to school, your teacher won't like you if you don't sit still."

"It's all right to watch that television program now, but when you start to school you'll be too busy to watch every day."

"You have to give up that filthy blanket before you start school. What would your teacher think of you with such a thing dragging behind?"

"What would your teacher say if she knew you wet the bed?"

If I were a five year old looking ahead to the twelve-year venture into the unknown, I could get enough of that kind of talk in a hurry. I realize your desire to help your child develop good habits, and I realize that as parents we often resort to almost anything in desperation. But we need to beware of the possibility of instilling in our children a sense of fear rather than a sense of trust even before they meet the object of their concern.

Instilling a Positive Attitude

On the positive side, there are some definite things you can do. For emphasis (positive reinforcement?), I will list these in a straight line to give you the idea of a check list so you can tick off what you have done.

1. *Tell exciting tales about the fun you had in school.*

Focus on the good times, the excitement, and the wonderful things you learned.

2. *Tell your child about your favorite teacher.*

In fact, why don't you sit down with your child and write your favorite teacher a letter thanking her for her inspiration and efforts. (I admit it; I'm sneaky. But it wouldn't hurt you to remember; it would warm the heart of your favorite teacher; and it would help your child feel positive about the teacher's role in his life.)

3. *When you help your prewriter draw pictures of his future teacher, draw her as a smiling, happy person.*
The teacher will get off to a much better start if your child doesn't begin school expecting her to be a person to be feared or dreaded.

4. *Help your child look forward to school by planning some exciting family activities to celebrate the event.*
In fact, if you want to do a good job of this, make a whole list of things that you and your child can do during every year of his school career. During first grade, you will read the *Narnia Chronicles* together. During second grade, you will build a model city together. During third grade, you can make a collection of pictures of state capitol buildings. During fourth grade, he gets to start guitar lessons. You get the idea.

You may want to keep your list fairly flexible, but there is value in building some anticipation for the event of another year. This may not help your child enjoy third grade at school any more, but it will at least give him something to look forward to. This activity is particularly important for the child who for some reason doesn't like school very much. The threat of twelve years of doing something he either doesn't enjoy or doesn't do well could be depressing.

5. *If you know of a child a year or so older than yours who is enjoying school, invite him over and engage him in conversation about his school experiences.*

This will help your child develop a sense of trust for the teacher and instill a feeling of expectation rather than dread.

6. *Help your child understand the differences in people.*

This may be a rather difficult teaching assignment, but you can point out to him that people have different demands and reactions. Use illustrations from friends and family. This will help him adjust to those various authorities he will meet during the school day.

The Really Practical Stuff

For the past forty Septembers, I have started to school in some capacity or another—student, teacher, principal. It really isn't a bad life, particularly if you happen to like yellow vehicles and the smell of new denim. But there is one aspect that never gets any easier, and that is readjusting the body clock to run on the school schedule.

School runs on schedule all right, whether the teachers and students are ready or not. Not only does the body have to be somewhere at a specific time, but the mind has to turn on and off according to someone else's routine.

The child in the first, second, or third grade who is adjusting to all this for the first time may not see the thrill of the challenge. You may have to help him. If your child is ever going to please enough people to be successful in school, you will need to help him understand this demand to be there when he is supposed to be. Here are some ways you can help him meet this challenge.

1. *Walk the route with your child.*

You can begin this emphasis by timing the journey to school before the term begins and he makes everybody angry by being a minute late. Comment about landmarks and potential dangers. (This is not just a suggestion for parents with first graders. Continue this practice with your child for several years.)

If your child is the kind of person who takes curious little side trips, allow a few extra minutes for such emergencies as a new dog on the block or roses in bloom. But get him out the door in time for him to make the journey.

Starting your child to school on time may require making some adjustments throughout the day. For example, you and the child will have to get up early enough to allow time for dressing emergencies, such as a button popping off or the shoes being left in the sandbox overnight.

You also need to allow enough time for your child to have a good breakfast. You have heard the sermon before, but it remains true. Every primary teacher I have ever met assures me that by nine-thirty she can pick out the children who have had a good breakfast.

2. Get your child to bed on time—starting well before school begins.

If all this early morning activity demands that you or the child get up a little earlier, you will have to compensate by going to bed a little earlier. This routine doesn't just happen with some psychological event called "Labor Day." You have to start a few weeks earlier preparing for it.

I realize it is tough to put an active six year old to bed while the August sun is still shining, but you can gradually lead into an earlier bedtime by planning some restful activities for the end of the day. Put the child in his room with books or drawing or counting. His body should get the message to rest. If your child is in the habit of an afternoon nap, you may want to help him gradually break into the routine of staying awake all day and going to sleep a little earlier in the evening.

If you suspect that your child is going to have difficulty resetting his body clock to the school schedule, it will help you to know what the school schedule is. Talk to the teacher and find out what is expected of the child at specific times during the day. Usually, primary teachers begin the day with either math or reading, depending on what the teacher thinks is most important. Most teachers feel that the early part of the morning is the choicest teaching time of the day.

3. Go light on the sugar at lunchtime.

Do your child's teacher a favor. An overdose of sugar can pump a lot of children into a state of immediate irrational energy at a time when the teacher is expecting them to sit silently while she reads an interesting book to the class. If your child comes home for lunch, you can control this with a balanced meal. However, if he takes his lunch, you may want to pack an orange instead of a Ding Dong. Since you don't know whether he is going to touch that peanut butter sandwich, you can at least prevent the possibility of his eating only sugar.

4. *Provide controlled after-school physical involvement and activities.*

School introduces the child to a new concept of body rhythms—the division of energies. There is physical energy and mental energy, physical exercise and mental exercise. When either of the energies is all spent, we are exhausted; but we might not always recognize why we are exhausted, so we don't know how to rest.

In normal situations, preschool children simply have more freedom of physical movement than they will have after they start school. Most children come equipped with a natural buzzer. They know when they have sat too long or have concentrated too long on some nonphysical project; so when they have the opportunity, they will get up and move around until they balance out the physical and mental energy levels.

But in the classroom, the child usually doesn't have the physical freedom to make that adjustment. Since schoolwork is predominantly mental, he spends his mental energy without sufficient physical breaks to keep the system in balance. Although the scheduled P.E. classes help, they simply aren't frequent enough to keep the child from becoming mentally exhausted.

Most experts advise college-age students—I repeat, college-age students—to keep their study minds alert by relaxing and exercising ten minutes out of every hour. No wonder the six year old wears out from the routines of first-grade learning.

When the child becomes mentally exhausted, he needs exercise, not inactivity. Some children know that naturally, and they will get their physical exercise. Oh, how they get their physical exercise! If your child is one of those who won't be cheated out of his physical movement, you may be a little shocked by his after-school behavior. You may find yourself asking such questions as: "What happened to my little lamb? He has always been so docile and quiet. Where is he learning all this stuff? Is school teaching him to be bad?"

If you get a rather abrupt change in behavior after your child starts school, you may want to check with the teacher just to make sure; but don't be surprised to find that this is just a natural reaction to his being mentally active and physically dormant for the past six hours.

Some children simply have more difficulty adjusting their bodies to the physical inactivity of school. If your child is having this problem, you may want to check with your family doctor. A few children do have a condition called hyperactivity.

In this case, the doctors usually prescribe a stimulant which slows the child down. But true hyperactivity is rare and can be difficult to diagnose. Don't accept just one opinion.

On the other hand, your child may react to his exhausting day by coming home, wolfing down a snack, and stretching out on the floor for six hours of passive television staring. Both children need the same therapy—physical activity. You can either appoint yourself the family recreation director in charge of walking, jogging, raking, biking, or building, or you may want to seek help from an outside activity (see Chapter 12).

5. *Make sure your child has some friends in his classroom.*

Since school learning takes place in a social context, the more comfortable the student is with that environment, the better equipped he will be to accept the vulnerability required to learn. He needs friends beside him. You can manage this. Find out who is in his class (the school will provide you with those names) and invite some students and their parents over to your house so the children can play together before school starts. I suspect that those parents will be happy to cooperate when they find out why you are doing this.

In the same way, if your child will be riding a bus, make sure he knows someone on the bus before school starts.

6. *Make sure your child knows his teacher before school starts.*

If that isn't possible, make sure the teacher and your child have a face-to-face conversation on one of the first days of the new school year. How do you engineer that? Easy! Make an appointment to pick up your child from his classroom on one of the first days of school. Thus, you will get to meet the teacher, you will get to see the room, and you can arrange a moment when your child and the teacher talk face-to-face.

You are going to give your child an idea of what school is like—whether you intend to or not. Without thinking, you can make school seem to be a fearful place. But with these few simple suggestions, you can do much to eliminate any pre-school jitters your child may be experiencing. With very little effort on your part, your preparation will ready him for an exciting new experience.

Homework Assignments for Parents

1. By your speech and behavior, what kind of image do you give your child about school?

2. What new things can you do to help your child get excited about his school? His teacher(s)? His friends?

3. Have you identified any changes in your child's behavior during the first few weeks of school? If so, have you determined what may be causing those behavior changes?

4. Have your child describe a typical day at school. Try to put yourself in his place and imagine what he is thinking and feeling at each moment.

SECTION 1: SCHOOL: A BRAND NEW WORLD

3

Inside the School Walls

o many parents, the school is an austere, alien monster that snatches up their children at nine o'clock every morning and spits them back at three-thirty every afternoon. I am not sure who is responsible for the chasm of misunderstanding that separates schools and parents, but I know it is unfortunate.

It seems as if the only thing the newspapers can print is how our schools are failing us. I've read those charges, too, but I can still claim that I am not afraid of schools. Before you write me off as a political activist, a nineteenth-century idealist, or an ostrich with his head stuck firmly in the sand, let me state my reasons.

First, I visit schools. I am in school more than 100 days a year. In one three-month period alone, I visited more than 200 classrooms in forty-three school buildings in four states. And guess what I found. I found warm, caring teachers who were working hard at providing every one of their students with a maximum learning experience. Oh, I found some bad ones, too; I won't lie to you. But I found enough good ones to give me confidence in what schools are doing.

Every parent needs to understand that caring teachers and loving parents have the same objective—to get the child through childhood and adolescence and into adulthood as a responsible, thinking, sensitive, moral, educated human. If you have any arguments with the school, those arguments will usually be about methods and techniques—about *means*, but rarely about *goals*.

If you will accept this point, you will be in a better position to help your child coordinate the two major influences in his life: family and school.

Apples for the Teachers

The key to the whole educational system is the teacher. Regardless of what the laws say, regardless of how the building looks, regardless of the quality of the textbook, the classroom teacher is the key to educational quality and direction. As far as your child is concerned, that teacher *is* the educational system. If he or she is sensitive and committed to the task of teaching, your child will find that the educational system is in fairly good shape. On the other hand, if the teacher is rude, incapable, or too tired to teach anymore, your child will find that education is in a sorry state.

I realize that this is an oversimplification of all the political and social powers and issues at work in our schools, but there are no laws nor administrative decisions that require teachers to be incompetent, insensitive, rude, arrogant, worldly, domineering, noncreative, dull, or intolerant of the child's convictions. If teachers display any of these characteristics, it is because they choose to do so.

If you are sincerely interested in helping your child make the most of his first three years in school, you will direct your attention to that individual classroom teacher. From my general observations, I find that some of the best teachers in the nation are assigned to the primary grades. In fact, many districts will assign only experienced, proven teachers to first grade. You just may find that the teacher, the key to educational quality, is your most capable helper in this task of rearing your child.

Even if your child ends up with a teacher whose methods or personality are not your ideal, the school year is not lost. Children have a wonderful ability to sort through, discern, forgive, and forget when forgetting is called for. In other words, they are resilient.

I have come to this belief from both teaching and parenting experiences. When I was a young teacher, I made a lot of mistakes. At times, I was downright stupid, and maybe even cruel. I still wake up in the middle of the night thinking about some of those blunders. For protection, I now try to avoid those towns where I spread my youthful incompetence. I don't want to go back and remind myself of how bad I was. I would prefer that those people never think of me at all.

But every now and again, some former student finds out where I have been hiding all these years. He calls me and invites himself and his family to come and remember old times. I shudder. I live in dread. I try to rationalize my youthful errors. I think about leaving town without a forwarding address.

But the day comes, the student arrives, and we have a great time. He never even hints that he remembers all those stupid incompetencies I plagued him with. If he does remember, at least he has not let those incidents destroy him. Could it be that his youthful resilience has blocked them out of his mind?

I see the same thing in my own children. Now that they are edging toward adulthood, they seem to have forgotten all the stupid things I did to them when they were younger. Or at least, if they haven't forgotten, they don't tell on me in front of my friends or my mother.

Sure, I know children get hurt. They are hurt by insensitive teachers, insensitive students, and insensitive parents. They are hurt by their own childish play. My first impulse, like yours, is to want to keep them from those hurts, to build a wall around them, to protect them from all suffering. But we can't do that, not realistically. Hurting is a part of life, so what we must do is to help our children endure the hurts they will inevitably encounter.

This point was emphasized to me one day as I was having lunch with a successful, well-adjusted young attorney. I asked him about his school experiences, specifically, which ones had been significant in making him the person he is.

To my surprise, he went all the way back to when he was in first grade. During the Christmas break, his family moved to another town. He started the new year at a new school, and he had the additional new responsibility of riding the bus home after school. He was an independent person, even in first grade, so he went out after school and got on the first bus that looked good. At each stop the bus made, he looked for his new house. But he couldn't find one that looked familiar.

When it got to the point where he was the last person on the bus, he began to worry. He knew he was lost, but didn't know what to do about it. He thought about hiding in the back of the bus, but realized it wasn't a good idea. Finally, he went up and told the driver of his predicament.

By this time, this lonely and frightened six-year-old child couldn't remember much except his new teacher's name. The bus driver returned to school, found the teacher, and she took her wandering student home to familiar surroundings.

The attorney explained to me that he learned two big lessons that first day of the second semester of first grade. First, he said he learned the lesson of survival. Later, in tight situations, he would recall his afternoon on the bus. If he could live through that, he could get through almost anything else. Second, he learned the lesson of receiving help. He had survived the experience because of a friendly, professional teacher. From then on, he knew that regardless of what happens, there is always someone somewhere who can provide help.

The System

The American educational system was designed to be a local operation. The founders of this country originally intended for the local communities to raise the money and make the decisions for their educational system. Thus, we have local districts, local school boards, and local property taxes. But in the interest of achieving some kind of uniformity and consistency, states established laws and agencies to make sure the local communities were doing their jobs well. So now we have state laws regulating such things as teacher certification, building safety, attendance policies, graduation requirements, selection of textbooks (in some cases), and school buses.

In recent years, the federal government has entered the scene, particularly with laws regarding the full rights of citizenship to all people regardless of race, sex, or ability. Now the federal courts have been assigned the primary responsibility of making sure the local districts comply with federal laws.

I offer this information in case you want to protest a policy or practice. In order to be effective, you will need to know at what level the decision was made.

Let me illustrate. Most states have a law that allows the school bus to pick up only those children who live farther than one and a half miles from school. If your first grader has to walk a mile, you may want to complain to the principal. But don't be surprised if you get nothing but sympathy. The school is only following a state law.

School years and school days are fairly uniform across the nation. Almost every state works on the basis of a 180-day school year, but this may fluctuate by as much as five days, depending on how the state counts teacher conferences. In most schools, the primary day is between five and five and a half hours. You may be interested in following some of the current discussion about lengthening both the school day and the school year. In several states, there is presently a general feeling that more is better.

Although this brief overview has not told you all you need to know about schools, it should help you realize that school is not a foreign country. It is simply an institution designed to support you in that awesome task of rearing your child. If you and the school can know each other well enough to cooperate on that assignment, together you should be able to provide a healthy climate for your child as he goes through this period of rapid growth and change.

Homework Assignments for Parents

1. How well do you know your child's teacher and school administrator(s)? Should you make an appointment to get to know them better?

2. Are you familiar with current state and local laws concerning your child's school? Where would you go to find answers to your questions? To register compliments or complaints? To find general information?

4

Learning Vulnerability and Conformity

A second-grade friend of mine recently missed three days of school because of an ear infection. I visited him the evening after his first day back at school. He showed me twenty-four work sheets he had been given to complete. Each sheet reviewed past concepts, presented a new concept, and drilled that new concept.

In three short days, my friend's classmates had learned at least twenty-four new concepts without him. Each of these concepts was important and needed to be learned before moving on the the next one. Some of these were concepts the child will use throughout his life.

That night I realized something again that I hope I never forget. The second grade world is a real world, filled with real pressures and real demands.

Imagine having to master an average of eight new concepts every day. Think what your life would be like if you missed even one of those concepts. You would have trouble mastering the lessons to follow. You could lose confidence in yourself. You might even tell yourself that you are dumb and that the work is too hard. Perhaps you would lose interest in even trying anymore.

School is a unique experience. It demands five hours of alertness. It demands social interactions. It demands conformity to rules and regulations. It restricts physical movement and demands that someone learn something. Of course, after a student has been around for a few years, he will probably become so used to the whole routine that he forgets that school is all that different from anything else, but it is still different.

Some people have called school a false experience. "If it were real," some educational experts declare, "students would have such a natural desire to learn that they would plunge into their studies so enthusiastically that all the educational problems would be solved."

I am reluctant to call school a "false experience." It may seem false to some adults who only visit on rare occasions, but to young people who are investing about a third of their waking hours in the place, school is the real world. For many children, school demands so much time and attention that it becomes the center of their entire world.

Consequently, as a parent of a school-age child, you must understand how the school experience is unique in the whole realm of human experiences, and how this unique experience dominates much of your child's time and emotions.

Learning in Public

One of the first things you must understand as you send that six year old off to school is the private character of learning. *Learning is a very intimate, personal process which demands from all learners a certain degree of vulnerability.* In order to learn, we first have to admit that we are inadequate, incomplete.

If we were perfect, there would be no need to learn. So before we can learn, we have to expose our inadequacy to those who propose to teach us. And if there are others around, such as in the classroom, we have to go through the agony of exposing our ignorance to them as well. At school, this private, personal activity of learning is put into a public arena.

I remember one time in the second grade when the teacher promised us extra recess time if we could make a perfect score on the weekly spelling test. For me, the test was a snap. I knew all the words forward and backward. But that was the problem: I spelled "not" as "ton."

What was my problem? Perhaps I was unmotivated. Perhaps I was careless. Perhaps I had not studied hard enough. Or perhaps my mind just took a short vacation as it occasionally does these days when I can't remember my own phone number. But whatever the reason, that kind of mental lapse during the first years of school can be hazardous to your grade, your reputation, your mental health, and your amount of recess time.

Even today, I don't mind being dumb. But I do hate to make it public knowledge, so I guard my ignorance with a passion. Am I any different from a normal second grader?

Learning is frequently an activity of trial and error. If we get something wrong the first time, we have to be emotionally prepared to keep trying until we get it right. That prospect alone is frightening enough; but when I think about the possibility of being wrong in front of twenty-seven of my classmates, I get weak knees. I can understand how students earn such teacher comments as "uncooperative," "inattentive," or even "lazy." It may be easier for a child to adopt one of those behaviors than to submit himself to the vulnerability of learning in a school setting.

Conformity vs. Individuality

In addition to struggling with the necessity of being vulnerable, a student in the first three years also has to struggle with the issue of conformity. Where at home he had been encouraged to express himself as a very worthwhile individual, at school he suddenly discovers the need to conform.

As one teacher told me the other day while considering the plight of education, "Students enter first grade as originals and come out of third grade as copies." It isn't a very promising possibility, is it?

I can remember one of *my* last truly original acts. I was in the third grade at the time. I had just spent the better part of a hot, sweaty afternoon working long multiplication problems, and I was ready for a break—or at least a word of encouragement. But when I took my paper up to show it to the teacher, she made those overdramatic gestures of displeasure (that teachers must practice for hours) and declared, "I just won't accept this. It is entirely too messy. I want you to separate those problems." So I did. I obediently took the paper back to my desk, got out my safety scissors, and separated those problems for her. That day I learned the penalty for being creative, and I haven't tried it since.

But does school have to be such a place? Is there any way that your child can adjust to the rituals and routines of school without losing his identity in the process? Let's hope so.

Too frequently when we speak of individuality or creativity, we put unnecessary limits on the concept. I define creativity here as the art of being inventive in thought or action. It is the process of taking what we know and then adjusting, extending, or applying it to whatever we are doing. The concept of creativity suggests that we are doing something out of the ordinary, but it does not necessarily imply that we are strange and bizarre. When we are being creative, we may just be putting some unusual twists to standard processes.

So now we need to ask ourselves, *Do schools refuse to accept such behavior? Is there something about the institution which prevents or discourages a child's creative urges?* I hope not; but at the same time, we have to admit that there are some characteristics about school life which make it a routine. And that routine can become so forceful that it represses creative bents. Let me list some of those characteristics.

1. *School requires conformity.*

Since your child is just one in a class of twenty-five or thirty, it is necessary for him to follow the rules that establish order and sameness in the class. If the teacher wants the child's name in a certain place on the paper, he must learn to put his name there. That not only teaches him to follow instructions, but it makes it easier for the teacher to read the paper. If the teacher wants the children to go to the bathroom in a straight line, your child will just have to learn to do so. If the teacher wants the books open to page thirty-five, your child will have to have his book open at page thirty-five. This isn't the time for him to be off fulfilling his own impulses to read what he wants to read.

2. *School emphasizes learning that can be measured, and we don't have very good ways of measuring inventive thought.*

Let's be honest. We talk about wanting our children to be creative, but first I want my child to learn to read, write, count, and add. When I go to see the teacher, I want her to tell me how my child is doing in those areas. I don't want to hear, "Although he's not learning to read, he does draw the most unusual pictures."

How is he doing in those areas of learning that can be measured? Schools are actually designed to teach those things. Teachers measure their success by how well their students perform in measurable activities. It is not as if schools actually discourage creativity. In fact, some teachers and some schools insist that they put a great deal of emphasis on this part of a student's development. But those learning skills that can be measured are more highly emphasized.

We may argue about whether that is the right emphasis, and we may even argue about who is to blame for the schools putting this kind of direction on their mission. Perhaps this is what schools do because this is what parents expect. Despite all this arguing, the student is going to be rewarded for learning things that can be tested, measured, and charted on a report card. There just isn't a lot of room for inventiveness in an activity such as spelling.

Of course, this kind of learning is not entirely contradictory to creative development. It just overshadows it in emphasis. In fact, we probably need those basic measurable skills in order to be more creative. We can't really create a new thought or project unless we have some learned base to use as a starting point. Thus, accumulating skills and knowledge will enhance a child's creative potential. But he will need some opportunity to see the prospect of doing something with that potential. At school he may not see that opportunity emphasized.

3. *School demands a lot of the student's time!*

Recently a parent called me to complain about his son's teacher. This parent felt that the teacher assigned so much homework that the child did not have time to explore his own imagination. When the parents consulted her, the teacher was shocked. She thought she was doing the children (and, subsequently, the parents) a favor by stimulating their intellectual growth.

I am not going to choose sides in this debate, but I do think every concerned parent should hear it. Homework is valuable, almost indispensable, in the education of your child. If your child is ever going to be completely proficient in such things as reading and computing math, he has to practice those skills outside of school. Regardless of how bright your child is or isn't, there simply is not enough time in school for him to master completely all the knowledge and skills you expect him to master. So on one hand, we thank the teacher for her care in making and marking homework assignments.

On the other hand, some teachers can get carried away with the homework routine. Not all work is good work. Not all work is worthy of the time it takes to do it. Some teachers do assign busywork to impress the students and parents.

Creativity needs time of its own. In fact, your child's creative genius may be most active when the rest of his body and mind is goofing off. Examples of this abound: The great scientist first thinks of his important principle while wading through the sand at the beach. The poet creates his masterpiece while lying in a rowboat looking at the sky. According to legend, the story of Frankenstein was created by a lady trapped in a cabin during a snowstorm. If these people had been out doing wholesome work, we might never have had discoveries which enrich our lives.

So now you have another conflict. You welcome the demands the school will put on your first, second, or third grader. You appreciate the fact that the teachers care enough to discipline their students' lives, concentrate on learning skills, and encourage students to study at home. At the same time, you want your children to have enough time, energy, and intellectual freedom to use their minds and hands for activities that can be called creative. You don't want your child to come out of third grade as just another copy.

Obviously, you are going to have to supplement the school in this area. You might wish that the school would provide children the stimulus and the reinforcement for their creative development, but I doubt that you can depend on that. If you want your children to develop and sustain their creative urges and impulses, you will have to help them.

Of course, in every chapter of this book I am encouraging you to supplement the school, but in this area it is particularly critical that you are prepared to help your child at home. In Chapter 15, you will discover some very specific activities you can use toward this end.

Homework Assignments for Parents

1. Do you encourage your child to be vulnerable as he learns at home? Do you try to prepare him for potentially uncomfortable learning situations at school?

2. Are you vulnerable with your child in regard to sharing easy-to-understand stories of your own failures and subsequent victories?

3. In what ways can you bridge the gap between the basics your child is learning at school and his individual creative gifts?

4. How can you help your child be creative during the times he doesn't really expect to be learning anything?

5

A Shift in Authority

Roger is a smart fellow, especially for a first grader. When he started school, he adapted quickly. He was gregarious with his fellow students, and he was always quite comfortable with teachers. In short, he soon became a class leader who perked up discussions, helped other students, and made the whole first grade a nicer place to be.

One day, about four weeks into the year, he went by himself to the school library to check out a book. When he came back to the classroom a little earlier than the teacher had expected, he was a different person. He was shy and rude. He isolated himself from the class, sat alone, and pouted defiantly. When the teacher tried to get to the root of the problem, Roger wouldn't say a thing.

Finally, about the time school was to be out, he motioned for the teacher. She thought maybe she would find out what was wrong. But all she could get from Roger was a stiff upper lip, some tears in the corner of his eyes, and a demand to call his mom. Concerned about his abrupt change of character, she accompanied him to the office.

When Roger couldn't get his mom on the phone, his internal hurricane broke loose with tears and shakings. Finally, in the comfort and protection of the nurse's office, the teacher managed to get an explanation.

It turned out that when Roger, the happy young man, went to the library, he had committed some minor breach of rules. The librarian had responded by yelling at him. Since Roger wasn't accustomed to such a rebuke, the surprise caused him to wet his pants, oh so slightly. That incident was the source of his afternoon behavior—another lesson in dealing with all the authorities in a first grader's life.

Who's In Charge Here?

When your child starts to school, he will meet new sources of authority and will have to adjust to another adult directing his activities. I don't want to put so much emphasis on this new experience that you feel like hiding your child in the closet, but I do want to make the point that this initial adjustment will have implications throughout your child's growing years. You need to spend some time thinking about this.

First, let us look at some of the possible problems that could mar this experience of starting to school.

1. *For the first time in his life, your child will have to submit to an authority figure who earned the office by some virtue other than love.*

First-grade teachers around the world will argue with this point, but let them argue. I am still right!

If you love your child (and I suspect you do, or you wouldn't be reading this book), he surely feels that love. Consequently, when you advise him or correct him or praise him, he knows that this advice and correction and praise were given out of love. He may not be able to identify that love, but acts of love are known through feelings rather than words anyway.

Yes, the teacher may love your child, too, but in a more impersonal way. So when the teacher advises or corrects or praises, the child has to understand some other context for that authority. It just isn't the same as when it comes from a parent. So what gives the teacher the right to this authority? Although the child may never be able to understand this in so many words, he still has to be able to sense it. Somehow he has to sense why adults other than his parents have a right and an obligation to order him about.

Just about the time he decides he can accept the teacher, he meets the teacher's aide, the principal, the janitor, the school nurse, the tester, and the lady in the lunchroom. He is thrown into a whole new dilemma of knowing which adults have authority for which specific areas of his life.

This is a critical time in a child's development. How he learns to respond to the roles of authority when he first meets them will have a great bearing on how he adjusts to school, how he adjusts to the whole learning arena, and how he adjusts to various sources of authority he will encounter during that time in his life when he must rely heavily on authority for what he is to do and even for what he is to believe. This leads us to the second problem.

2. *You must have a clear understanding about how you want your child to respond to authority.*

As a teacher, I can assure you that there is no guarantee that your child is going to turn out exactly as you want him to. In the process of creation, the Infinite Mind saw fit to give the child some voice in this matter. In other words, God made him an individual. But you need to know what lessons you are trying to teach your child. Also, since those lessons are most forcibly taught through modeling, you must understand how you respond to authority.

Do you teach your child an unquestioned acceptance of every adult's advice or correction? Do you teach him to fight against all authority, responding to nothing except his own conscience? Or do you teach your child to consider the source, think through the evidence, and make a rational decision about which authority he will accept and which he will ignore?

Again, let me assure you that just in the process of living and being, you are teaching your child one of those positions (or perhaps some combination of all three). But you are nevertheless teaching him to respond to authority in some way. Although he may not do it your way, you must be sure that the message you are communicating is the one you want your child to learn.

3. *For the first time in his life, your child may face conflicting authorities.*

Let's suppose, for example, that you are from the old school which believes little children should refer to adults with some degree of formality. About the time you get this message across to your six year old, he starts to school, and the first-grade teacher wants to be called Sally. Now what does he do? What do you do? For months you have been pumping this child up to accept the authority of his teacher, and now she contradicts you.

This may call for a scene. You can begin with your child. You can try to explain Sally's peculiar idiosyncrasy, telling him that some adults may prefer being addressed by the first name, but all adults will accept the last name with the appropriate title. If you are good at explaining, and your child is good at accepting, this may suffice. But I doubt it. When one is six years old there is something rather romantic and brazen and grown-up about calling some adult, particularly an adult with authority, by his or her first name. Don't be surprised or disappointed if your child seems to like the idea.

So now you have two options. You can insist that your child obey your wishes, or you can go see Sally. You do have a right to both. You have a right to insist that your child accept your principles of authority. You may have to insist several times before he gets the message; but usually, if the matter is significant enough to justify confrontation in the first place, it is worth your effort to keep reminding the child of your rules until he remembers them.

On the other hand, I urge you to go see the teacher. As a parent, you must realize and affirm that all those other adults and adult authorities in your child's life are your helpers in the enterprise of getting your child through childhood and adolescence into adulthood. They are helpers, nothing more; and they gain the right to their authority by your implied permission.

These helpers must understand that they are helpers. They don't have the principal responsibility in this endeavor. They only have the child for a limited time, so they must work within the framework of a much broader scheme. So long as your agenda for your child is not immoral or illegal, those helpers have to honor your program.

As a teacher, Sally has to understand that, and you may have to remind her. If she doesn't believe you, tell her to call me and I will tell her. Teachers must honor the parents' wishes for their children, so long as those wishes are based on sound judgment and human decency and do not disrupt the classroom climate.

Of course, I use the story of Sally only as an illustration. This problem of conflict of authority in your child's life can rear its ugly head in several places. If you are a thinking parent, trying to rear your children according to the principles of

Scripture, you are going to meet this problem frequently. For example, Halloween has always been a source of frustration for our family. What do you say to a seven year old just after you have told him that he cannot go trick-or-treating regardless of what all the other kids, and the teacher, are doing that night?

Every family has its own rituals, its own cultural rules, its own agenda, and its own value structure. When your child first wanders out into the bigger world away from the security of that limited culture, he is going to bump into some conflicting rules. You will have to help him manage those.

4. *At this age, your child will look to authority not only to tell him what to do and how to behave, but also to tell him what to believe.*

This is simply the way the human belief structure works for most of us. When we are young, we believe what we do because our accepted authority told us to believe it. Later, we will probably question that authority, and then we will reaffirm those beliefs on a different basis. But for a while, those beliefs by authority serve us well.

Usually, your child will accumulate a whole trunkful of those during his first three years in school. He will develop some beliefs about his nation and his duty to country and fellowman. He will develop some beliefs about the value of education and the definition of success. And, if he has been reared in a typical evangelical home, he might initiate a personal relationship with his Savior.

Those are some rather serious beliefs he is picking up at the same time he is trying to sort through all those sources of authority which have just entered the picture. During this time, your child is going to need you to help him coordinate all the active advice and all the models he is getting so he can form a healthy attitude toward authority.

Getting to Know Your Child's Teacher

It's important to establish a working, healthy, productive relationship with the teacher. Aaugh! At this, you may be tearing at your hair and shrieking about my naiveté. You may even accuse me of being an idealist. After all, you have been around teachers before and are convinced that they are too self-sufficient, arrogant, and complacent to be interested in talking to parents.

Let me assure you. That is only a front. Teachers are as frightened of parents as parents are frightened of teachers. Do your child a favor. Break down that barrier. Help your child's teacher be a success with at least one student.

It is important for you to know your child's teacher. Know what she is like, what her values are, what motivates her, what amuses her, what angers her, and how she responds to various situations. Since you are turning your child over to this helper for about a third of his waking hours, you have every right to know these things about that helper. You need to know, not only for your own peace of mind, but so you can assist and supplement when necessary.

At the same time though, that helper (teacher) needs to know those same things about you. You wouldn't hire an assistant to help you with your life's number one project without giving that person some orientation. In the same way, that teacher needs to know you so she can help you in the mission of rearing your child. Don't keep her in the dark. Make sure she knows who you are and what you expect.

Here are some suggestions:

1. *Go to school and meet the teacher on her turf.*
See her in person. Sit down and chat for a few minutes. You don't have to be conspicuously frank during that first meeting. If she is any student of psychology at all (and how else could she have made it through teacher training?), she can make some observations and read between the lines. She will discern what you feel is important.

Also, make sure your child knows you are conversing. In fact, I recommend having the child present at the teacher conferences. This way the child will get the idea that the teacher and parent respect each other, and he will be more open to accepting both authorities in his life.

2. *Invite the teacher to your house or to a restaurant so she can meet you on your turf.*
Turnabout is fair play. Of course, this

suggestion comes from the teacher part of me instead of the parent part, but there is great possibility here. With salaries what they are in most places, many teachers would appreciate an invitation to a free lunch or an after-school snack. This will give your child the opportunity to see the authorities in his life sit informally and chat about such profound topics as soufflé recipes and Superbowl scores.

Any friendly conversation between you and your child's teacher could have an enormous effect on his attitude toward the teacher and his whole approach to learning. Don't deny yourself this rather simple method of enhancing your child's school experience.

3. *If you have some extra time, see if you could spend some of it at school on a regular basis.*
Many schools have developed various programs for encouraging volunteer help. If your school has some kind of program, volunteer. If not, suggest one. Don't hide behind your feelings of inadequacy. You can help supervise the lunchroom, listen to second graders read, or do some filing for a teacher. This is something for you to do. In addition to the value you will be to the school and the children you help, your own child will get the idea that you approve of school and what is happening to him. Also, you will be able to relate his tales of school to specific scenes and people. Then when he tells you about Jason marking up the bulletin board, you will be able to visualize the crime.

Growing is always an exciting business, but we must remember that as we grow into something, we also grow out of something. The give-and-take inherent in growth is probably never more obvious than during the time when you and your child learn to manage the other authorities in his life.

We have research and biblical admonition telling us that what parents do, children repeat—maybe not in every case, but often enough to be sobering. If you regularly yell at referees, policemen, and bosses, don't expect too much different from your child. If you want your child to respect authority, demonstrate it for him. Then he will more readily transfer that respect to teachers, administrators, and other authority figures throughout his lifetime.

Homework Assignments for Parents

1. How have you prepared your child to encounter authority figures other than parents/relatives?

2. As your child sees your response to authority, what lessons is he learning?

3. In what area(s), if any, do you foresee problems concerning your child's attitude toward authority?

4. Given the amount of (or lack of) free time you have, to what extent can you get involved in your child's school/activities? What can you do to increase the quality and/or quantity of that time?

SECTION 2:
THE FOUR R'S

Reading

⊄ [£ √ * ? £] § [£ %   ∩ [£   ] ∪ £   π >   > * < £

> ∪ = =   π >   • π ø   ∩ π   ) £   ] = * < £

*   π ⊂ £ √ £ %   + ø   + * √ %   ∩ π   > * = =   ]
      = * > £ = π √ ∪   √ £ £ %

*   = £] ? √ £ %   ∩ π   ? £] %

Did you enjoy my poem? Or did you find it
frustrating because you couldn't make
any sense out of those scratches? (If you
want to know what it says, see the solution at the
end of this chapter.)

This is just a glimpse of what your child goes
through when he moves from a nonreading
world into a reading world. The "simple" process
of interpreting and digesting those written
scratches is the single most important intellectual
activity in the modern world. If your child is ever
to become educated, if he is ever to succeed in a
world so dependent on such symbols, if he is ever
to become an intelligent shopper in the grocery
store, if he is ever to develop a personal
devotional life based on Scripture, if he is ever to
travel on the highways, if he is ever to go places

he has never been before, if he is ever going to know the joy of entertaining himself through the pages of a good book, he needs to become proficient at the skill of reading.

Reading: A Learned Activity

Most children, with proper instruction, supervision, and encouragement, can learn to read as well as they want or need to read. The rare exceptions are those very special children who have learning disabilities that prevent them from performing one of the brain operations required in reading. But if your child is normal, he can learn to read.

How well he reads could depend on how well he is taught and encouraged. For this reason, those first three years are crucial for him, for you, and for his teachers. The three of you need to cooperate in this adventure so that your child can master the skill sufficiently to achieve his creative potential.

How well your child does during those first three years will have significant impact on how well he does throughout his educational career. To help your child make this transition into a reading world, you need to understand as much as you can about the process of reading. Let me offer some thoughts.

1. *Reading is saying words.*

At its most fundamental level, reading is saying words. It combines the process of seeing the letters, sounding them out, putting the accent in the right place, and making a word. Of course, as a child improves, he moves through this stage rather rapidly. The whole process becomes almost automatic for an experienced reader. But it is still a necessary, fundamental procedure.

A few years ago, one of my superiors asked me to read a report he had written. It was a solid piece of work, but the conclusion just didn't make any sense. Finally, the man asked my opinion. I shuddered at the possible consequences of being too honest, and told him what I thought. He acted shocked and only mildly upset, so I asked him to read the conclusion to me. When he read it aloud, it sounded all right. So I checked it again and found the problem—one small word. The word was supposed to have been *now,* and he was reading *now.* He had always read *now*—but the typist had typed *not.* This may be a minor difference in spelling, one small letter, but it sure makes a ton of difference in meaning.

Regardless of how proficient we become in the skill of reading, we still need to say the words occasionally. You don't want to dwell on this; it is very basic. But you do want to give your child opportunities to read aloud.

2. *Reading is imaging.*

One of the reasons we read is to take the words from the paper and use them to sketch a picture in our minds. When your child sees the word *snake* and says the word *snake,* he draws a picture of a snake in his mind. If he has never seen a snake, he may need some other cues to help him get the picture right. You may have to show him a picture or go into some description. Frequently without those added cures to help guide him to the image, the reader will just skip over the word as if it isn't even there. That is an interesting little tool most of us use occasionally—the ability to skip over a word, either written or oral, for which we don't have the sufficient background to decipher. But it can be dangerous practice, particularly for a beginning reader.

Imaging through reading is still one of the most rewarding and cheapest pleasures available to us. I will never forget Huck Finn's raft or Heidi's home in the mountains because I built those pictures in my own mind from the words the authors used. Don't disturb me with some movie. My image is too much a part of my memory.

I urge you not to cheat your child out of such pleasures. Read to him and let him read to you. Show him how to build those pleasant and memorable images.

3. *Reading is receiving information.*

One of the functions of reading is to get the facts off the paper and into our brains. Although this is not completely different from imaging, it does require a bit more precision. In imaging, if the word is *dog,* the child can imagine any dog, but if the sentence tells the reader that the basenji doesn't bark, the reader has to be more precise in handling the data. And being precise requires more activity from the reader. Unless the author has been very elaborate with his structure, the reader has to build some structure for grasping and grouping the facts. In order to store the information, he has to put it into some kind of mental package, and usually the reader is responsible for providing that package himself.

When the child begins to read for the purpose of acquiring information, he will probably need some help in such activities as distinguishing between important and unimportant material. He will have to recognize the topic sentences, and he will need a concept of outlining or categorizing. These are rather sophisticated tools for the average eight year old.

4. *Reading is interacting.*

Recently I read this statement: "The word *education* comes from the Latin verb *educare* meaning 'to lead out'; so the appropriate education is that which leads out of the student what he already knows but doesn't know he knows." At that point I stopped and said to myself, "Wait a minute. I'm not sure I agree with that. I have some arguments that will have to be answered before I can accept that definition." So I kept reading to see if the author was smart enough to answer my questions and convince me of his definition. I was interacting with the material.

To become intelligent readers, we must learn to interact with the material. We must learn that all written material is not necessarily true or infallible, that it has to stand the test of our own thoughts and feelings. And we must learn that we have to reflect on some of our written material.

Notice that I used the word *learn* in each of the above warnings. I did so on purpose. Interacting is a learned skill that is often a little late in arriving. Try walking into a sixth-grade class and announcing that there is a mistake in the students' textbook. That ought to get an argument started in a hurry. "What do you mean, a mistake in the book? Who do you think you are to question the book? I don't care what you say. I am going to memorize it exactly as it is written because that is what the teacher wants on the test." Oh, the protests are endless!

But that kind of reading, reading only for information without interaction, can lead to the danger of accepting at face value everything in newspapers, magazines, or books. Somewhere in his reading development, your child will need to learn to interact with the material.

Steps in Learning to Read

The four points above constitute my analysis of what happens when we are reading. Although you might get a different approach from someone else, please see my intent. As a parent, you have to understand what is happening in your child's mind as he begins and develops his reading skills. An analysis of reading can provide you the direction for that understanding, and it can also lead to the next question: What are the steps or stages in learning to read?

Step 1: Readiness

Not all children mature at the same age. For some unexplained reason, some are ready to read earlier than others. This has absolutely nothing to do with intelligence, parenting, or destiny. It is a matter of fact.

Some children learn to read at a very early age. In fact, there is a heavy dose of material available which suggests that almost all children can learn to read at three. That may be true. Perhaps they can learn to read, but I am not sure I understand why they or their parents want them to. If a child has a natural desire, then he will learn on his own. Otherwise, I see no reason to force a child into reading before he has a social need (school) for the skill.

To affirm this conviction, I made a thorough study of the issue. (I talked to ten people.) But I did select good ones. I picked the ten most scholarly people I know—people who read widely and effectively, and who use their reading as a research tool—and asked each, "At what age did you learn to read?"

The reaction was similar for all, men and women alike. "Oh, I don't really remember. It was sometime after I had started the first grade, though." This convinced me. If these people could start reading in the first grade and become scholarly, there is no need to force a child into reading at any earlier age.

I do suspect that most children can be forced to read before they are ready, but I also suspect that they will approach the task with something less than intense enthusiasm and will perform according to that level. Perhaps one of the easiest and most effective ways to help a child move into a reading world is to help him develop a readiness for the activity.

Obviously, there needs to be a physical readiness. The child has to be strong enough to hold the book, and he has to be able to focus his eyes on the page. He needs adequate self-control to sit still long enough to get a message from the material. He has to have some understanding that the material contains a message that's worth his time and effort to acquire. He has to be able to remember an image. Some of these functions can be learned.

Although kindergarten curriculum and aims fluctuate greatly from school to school, most kindergarten programs are designed to move the child toward a readiness for reading. Nevertheless, you still need to assist in the endeavor. There are several things which you can do.

First, and probably most important, read to your child. Start this early and continue it faithfully for as long as you both can still enjoy it. I know families where the father still reads to his family on regular occasions even after the children have reached high school age. (In every case, those are solid families. *I wonder . . . .*) From your reading sessions, your child will learn several lessons. He will learn that books carry worthwhile, entertaining messages; he will develop some control of his body; and he will learn that you care about him.

Second, if you have questions about selecting the right material, go see your local librarian. As soon as your child is old enough to walk, take him to the library, get him a card, introduce him to the children's librarian, and request her help in selecting the appropriate material. Librarians are not only trained in such matters, but every one I have met is critically interested in building good reading habits in children. I suspect your librarian will be very happy to help you, and library service is quite reasonable. You can afford this investment in time even if you can't afford to buy books.

Third, while you are reading to your child, allow enough time to involve him in the process. Let him look at the pictures first and see if he can anticipate the story. Stop occasionally and show him a particular word. Let him imagine the scene for you. He may even draw it. But whatever you do, make reading an active process for your child.

If you feel a bit overwhelmed or awkward with all these suggestions, don't worry. I suspect that most parents feel the same way when they first start the endeavor. At least, I did. But we must rely on the child's sense of understanding our intentions. Even if you make all the mistakes in the world, just making an attempt will be a significant stimulus in moving your child toward readiness—and it is never too late to start. Even if your child has already grown out of the first three years of school and is in the fourth or fifth grade, try reading to him anyway. You both may find the sessions quite rewarding.

Step 2: Recognizing the Sounds of Letters

When I list this as one of the early stages of learning to read, some of the experts will boo and hiss, but others will shout, "Amen!" Although I realize that not everyone agrees on the role of the study of phonics in learning to read, I am convinced of its importance.

For the past several years, I have taught college seniors. During that time, I have discovered that those who learned phonics usually have fewer problems in spelling, word formation, and reading than those who didn't. Besides, I am not sure I understand the reasons for the debate. Learning phonics is a rather simple procedure which surely merits the time your child will spend on it. Yet your child's teachers may not be thoroughly convinced. Consequently, you may need to be ready to help your child in this area (provided I have convinced you of its importance).

You can begin by making some flash cards. These don't have to be flashy. In fact, the homemade kind may be more interesting. Turn the cereal box inside out and cut it into little squares. Your child may learn to read by studying both sides. When he can pronounce *riboflavin*, he is ready to go on to bigger things.

Make flash cards with letters, with letter combinations, and with words. After you have introduced your child to a sound such as *d,* show him a couple of words that have a *d* sound at the beginning and perhaps at the end. You can still work on the sound as he gets familiar with hearing it in a word. Some of the educational television programs try to make this flash card idea more memorable by giving each sound a personality. If you feel dramatic, you may try techniques such as this.

From the flash cards, you can move into books. Have your child pick out certain letters he recognizes. Very soon he will be pronouncing the words themselves.

You may also want to move him into writing at this stage. While you are still working with the flash cards, you can pronounce the sound and have him write the symbol. This will be the ultimate test of whether he is mastering this particular symbol and sound.

Let me add here that these steps or stages are not necessarily in order. Your child can read and perhaps even read well without a full knowledge of phonics. Don't discourage his reading, but use the phonics study as a supplement.

Step 3: Recognizing the Words

With a solid background in phonics, your child should be able to develop good skill in deciphering words, including those not in his reading vocabulary. Of course, phonics is not a foolproof method, because English words don't always sound as they are supposed to, but it is still a good tool. Again, I would be reluctant to be overly critical of a child's mispronunciation so long as he is being accurate with his phonic reasoning. Learning to read requires taking some risks, so be as positive as possible while the child is still in the beginning stages.

Again, you may want to try the flash cards with words. You can make games out of these. The other day I visited a home where every piece of furniture and ornament was wearing a brightly colored name tag. When the five year old came in, I got a guided tour, not only of the furniture but also of his newly acquired words.

At this stage of your child's development, the most important thing is to have him read to you. But you have to listen and watch closely. He can develop some bad habits here. Watch for such things as transposition—changing the letters around and getting the wrong word. For example, *dog* becomes *god*. Also watch for the potentially bad practice of skipping words. I have known high school students who were particularly hindered by this habit. Make sure your child reads carefully enough to distinguish each letter. Remember the *not* and *now* illustration I used earlier. But the most important thing is to make sure the child is getting the meaning from the context.

Listening to your child read may not be as inviting as watching "M*A*S*H" reruns, but it is absolutely essential at this stage. Learning to read requires some trial and error and risk taking, and someone has to listen to your child as he goes through this procedure. Although his teacher means well, and I am sure she is doing the best she can, she simply does not have time to listen to every child read as much as he should. If you want your child to read well, you must listen to him during those first three years while he is perfecting the skill and building habits. And once you have started this practice, you just may want to continue it for several years.

Step 4: Reading for Images, Insights, and Meaning

Even before your child becomes proficient at saying the words, he is also ready to learn that reading is an exciting, entertaining, informative activity. The kind of reader he becomes depends on how well he learns that lesson. If he learns it well, he will have the motivation to read a lot. As he reads a lot, he will become a better reader. There really aren't any shortcuts at this stage. A reader who reads well is one who has read a lot.

Of course, if you took my advice about using the library, you have already begun to teach your child this important lesson. You have shown him that books are valuable. Through your reading to him, you have shown him the entertaining feature of the activity. So you're well on your way, but you still need to encourage him. Some suggestions follow.

First, you can *put some importance into his reading.* Give him some responsibility. Have him read the road signs when you travel. Have him check the movie ads in the paper to see where his favorite show is playing. Make sure he gets some mail, even if you have to bribe someone to write to him. Introduce him to the use of reading as a tool in such things as math, art, and science. Let him read the instructions while you assemble his new bike.

Second, *make sure his mind is active while he is reading.* How do you do that? You discuss his reading with him. This isn't bad dinner table conversation, so make it a common practice. All through his school career, your child will need that kind of interaction with you and with his reading. Not only will you stay in touch with his reading development, but you can also keep in contact with his whole intellectual and spiritual growth.

Finally, at this stage you need to *provide your child with the environment conducive to reading—a comfortable place free from outside stimuli.* In other words, you may have to turn off the TV, put the video games in the drawer, and put the Barbies or cars to rest. This may not be as easy as it sounds.

Although you may have provided your child with his own room for that very purpose, don't be surprised if he is the kind of person who would rather be with the family. Who wants to go off to an old, cold room to read when all the family warmth and love is somewhere else? So you may have to turn that warmth-and-love room into a reading environment for a while.

Step 5: Improving Speed

I am almost reluctant to include this as a stage in reading development because I am not convinced that slow reading is always much of a liability. Sometimes it may even be an asset. However, some children have some bad habits that can and should be corrected. If the child continues the practice of pronouncing each word, either aloud or silently, he will never achieve a satisfactory speed. Improving this is mostly a matter of reminding and correcting.

After a child learns to read silently, reading speed becomes largely a matter of eye focus— enlarging the space on the page the reader sees at any instant. There are some rather sophisticated machinery and exercises designed to improve eye focus. If you feel that your child needs to increase his reading speed, you may want to check with his teacher or with a professional reading consultant. Your school district may have such a person on staff.

Learning to read is a rather mysterious activity that can have a very significant effect on your child's whole intellectual development. If you are a caring parent, I urge you to care enough to supervise this process.

Homework Assignments for Parents

1. Does your child enjoy reading? Why or why not?

2. What specific things are you doing to foster your child's desire to read?

3. How are you helping your child with pronunciation? Forming images? Receiving information? Interacting with written material?

4. At what stage is your child in the learning-to-read process? What is the next step he needs to take?

When I reached the age of five,
Full of joy to be alive,
I opened my mind to fill a lifelong need;
I learned to read.

7

Writing

When a child enters the first grade, he barely knows how to hold a pencil while he draws his name. When he comes out of the third grade we expect him to be an accomplished author.

We expect a big chunk of growth and development to be crowded into three short years. Like reading, writing is a learned, personal skill that requires individual supervision and direction.

If you want your child to develop the right skills and attitudes toward the two dimensions of writing—penmanship and expression—you will have to assist the teacher. Most teachers simply do not have enough time to provide each child with enough encouragement and feedback to sufficiently match his or her rate of learning. That's where the parent can be a valuable help.

To be of greatest assistance to your child, you need to understand both the writing process and your own child's special level of maturity. To get a better idea of what your child is going to experience, let's study those two dimensions as separate skills.

Penmanship

Most children make rapid progress in the simple skill of making intelligent marks on paper. They have to, because we expect rapid progress in this area. We expect them to move from pencil holding through primitive drawing into cursive writing in three years.

To start with, penmanship is not all that natural as a skill. There is probably no other physical activity quite like the activity of holding a pencil and making it operate the way we want it to. When the child first reaches the age when he begins writing, he has probably not had any previous experience that will help him master the art. The act of writing requires the child to use a new set of muscles in a different way.

Frequently, five- and six-year-old children simply don't have the muscular maturity to hold the pencil the way we would like them to hold it, so they learn to compensate. To see how original children can be in learning to compensate for their muscular immaturity at that stage, visit my class of college seniors and look at all the varieties of pencil holding and letter construction among those young adults. All are still using skills they learned during their first three years of school.

Although the penmanship experts disagree about the correct way to hold a pencil and about what to do with the child who manages incorrectly, the general feeling is that if the child is succeeding at his unique style, we should leave him alone.

Of course, there are some specific ways to help him.

1. *Get your child an oversized pencil.*

Most of the child's physical activity up to this point has been big-muscle movement. Writing requires precise small-muscle movement. At this stage, a fat pencil is easier to grasp and direct. As the child improves his small-muscle control, he will soon grow out of his need for that oversized pencil and you can move him to the regular size.

In fact, you can make a reward out of this. Order him a pencil from Disneyland or some other exotic place, and present it to him when he masters the skill of pencil control. That should bribe him into practicing.

2. *When the child is first learning the art of holding and directing the pencil, don't discourage his spontaneous creations.*

Let him practice controlling the pencil to make what he wants to make. Don't put too many limits on him by insisting that he write his name or something significant. Any practice in pencil control is valuable. If your child likes to imitate, draw a lot of designs for him—circles, lines, letters, numbers—and let him control the pencil. Encourage him to draw pictures.

3. *If your child needs help making the correct symbols (letters or numbers), seek creative solutions.*

One idea is to buy him a set of letter blocks and have him practice by tracing his finger through the letters. You might also stand behind him as he is sitting at his desk, put your finger in the middle of his back, and trace a letter. This will usually transfer over into his hand. This technique is particularly valuable if your child is getting some little part of a letter wrong such as putting the hump on the wrong side of the letter *p*. (Incidentally, I first encountered these two techniques while reading the educational theories of Quintilian, a first-century Roman. Obviously, children and penmanship have not changed all that much in the last two thousand years.)

4. *Break down the task of writing into manageable parts.*

If you show your child the number 5, he may get overwhelmed with the size of the task. But if you show him a straight line across, a straight line down, and a little curl on the bottom, he should be able to imitate that.

Actually, this is an important teaching theory for any study at any age. If we tell ourselves that we can't learn something, we are usually overwhelmed with the total picture. If someone breaks it down into manageable parts for us, we can learn those parts, put them together, and master the task.

To prove this is true, I, a world-class klutz, learned to juggle the other day. Imagine that! This guy who keeps daily records by soup stains on his tie instead of a diary, juggles. It is actually rather simple—just a series of individual hand movements that can be learned one by one.

Do your child a favor. Break his penmanship task down into distinct, manageable hand movements.

5. *Practice, practice, practice.*

If you are committed to helping your child practice during that special time when he is learning to print his letters, please check with his teacher. There are so many different styles of printing lurking around first-grade classes that you will need to know what and how he is being taught at school. Many of these more recent styles of printing are designed to look like cursive so the child will not have as much difficulty making the transition from printing.

Since penmanship is a physical skill, the key to learning and improving is the same as in any other physical skill—practice and feedback. To make the practice palatable, give the child some practical, real chores that require him to write. Encourage him to practice his penmanship through his desire to express himself.

Expression

Although learning to hold a pencil and make intelligible marks on paper may not be a natural skill, it is worth learning because we need to express ourselves. We need some means to say what we think. We need some way to share our feelings and ideas. We need some method for convincing and persuading other people of our position when we know we are right.

If you can convince your child of the value of writing as a means of expression, you will probably produce a good writer, competent both in penmanship skills as well as the skills of written expression. Actually, competent expression is more of an attitude anyway. Good writing grows out of confidence. If the person is confident that he has something worthwhile to communicate, he will almost always find the means to express himself.

From the very beginning, the child should be convinced that he is learning these skills so he can share his ideas with a wider audience. In fact, it is rather common and perhaps healthy for the more confident children to become frustrated with their written language skills at the early stages. They really want to say more than they have the tools to say.

One of the tests to see whether you have done a good job of creating a positive attitude toward writing is to count how many times your child bothers you to spell words for him. Usually, this is a good sign for a first, second, or third grader. It indicates that he understands the value of the written language. Whatever you do about all the pestering, don't discourage that attitude. It will be valuable to him throughout his school career.

How do you foster that attitude? Some of it may be natural to particular children. But some of it can be developed, and this is what you can influence. You can begin early, about as soon as the child becomes competent in oral language.

1. *Have your child dictate to you—a story, a poem, a letter to Grandmother—while you write it for him.*

Show him the work. Have him read it himself, often. Let him see what he has created. Remind him of the time when he will be old enough to eliminate your role in the process. Make this a regular practice, and keep it going well into his school career. As he becomes competent in writing, he can be the steno while both of you dictate. Teach the child not to be afraid of his own mind.

2. *After he learns to write, read what he has written.*

Writing is a form of expression. The very definition suggests that somebody read and interact with what we have written. When I put the finishing touches on this chapter, I plan to put on my boots, walk a mile through fourteen inches of snow to my wife's office, and demand that she read it. I want feedback and I want it now. Besides, I know she will be sensitive, even if she doesn't agree with everything I have said.

Although your seven year old may not be as childish as I am, he still appreciates interest in what he has written. If you show interest, he will write more. Again, since teachers are busy, they may not have enough time to provide your child with as much feedback as his writing deserves. Just to make sure, assign yourself the task.

3. *Make some games out of your child's writing skills.*

Your second grader is probably capable of publishing a family newspaper, but you may have to give him the idea. A production of an original musical comedy played in the backyard for all the local dogs and neighbors would not only fill a summer afternoon, but would also provide an opportunity for your child to exercise some writing skills.

Such activities in written expression can teach your child several valuable lessons. Through these, he can develop a sense of confidence, and this confidence will help him develop his creativity and imagination. Since writing demands sense awareness, the child will learn to be more astute as a listener and observer.

Sometimes simple drills in listing sensory feedback is an excellent writing activity. Take your child to the park. When you get home, have him make a list of the sounds and smells and sights he remembers. Single words in a straight line are sufficient. He will learn the lesson of expression.

4. *Encourage him to observe in some kind of order.*

Writing is also an excellent activity to teach the skill of organization—of organizing thoughts and images and ideas so that they can be filed in the mind for future use or they can be communicated in an orderly fashion.

The skill of organization is one of the most valuable skills a person can master. If you can help your child develop it, you will have performed a great service. You can begin this even during the prewriting days when the child is still dictating his stories to you. Have him send a description of his room to his grandmother, but make him see it in order. When he tells you a story, help him get the events in chronological order. If he has an idea, help him put it into an outline. Incidentally, that skill of organization will ultimately lead to the skill of outlining, and outlining is a must for any effective, productive writer or speaker.

Written expression not only demands basic knowledge of the language, it also *teaches* the language. The best way to teach such things as vocabulary, spelling, or sentence construction is to have the child write. Be prepared to answer his questions. Be prepared to make suggestions for improvement. (Regardless of what some language experts tell us, I still feel a word spelled correctly communicates more than a misspelled word.) If you are not totally confident in your own ability in punctuation, capitalization, or other points of usage, invest in a good grammar handbook. *The Plain English Handbook,* written by the Walshes and published by Random House-McCormick-Mathers, still sells for less than five dollars. It lists all the rules in a neat order so you can get to them quickly.

As I said at the beginning of this chapter, good writing is more of an attitude than a skill. If your child has enough confidence in himself that he wants to share his ideas, he will probably learn the skills needed to achieve his goals.

Homework Assignments for Parents

1. Specifically, what things are you doing to help develop your child's penmanship? What else do you need to do to encourage him?

2. Have you recognized your child's need to express himself? How strong is his inclination to be expressive?

3. Do you ever give off signals that might make your child wary about coming to you for help in developing his skills? How can you avoid such negative feedback?

4. Are you sure to provide more praise than criticism as your child begins to learn to write? If not, what are some things you can compliment right away to help him feel good about himself?

8

Math

In the areas of reading and writing, you have to watch your child to see that he doesn't form bad habits. In math, you have to watch to see that he doesn't form bad *attitudes*. Bad math habits that hinder his progress can usually be corrected. But if he gets turned off to math or thinks it is beyond him, that attitude can haunt him the rest of his life. To help you be alert to that danger, I present three characteristics of elementary mathematics learning.

Young Children Are Concrete Thinkers

At the ages of six to eight, children think about *things*. They aren't much good at thinking about ideas, theorems, or abstractions. If you can remember this while your child is young, you might turn yourself into a fair math teacher.

The principle is simple. Teach your child by using things. Teach him to count things. Teach him to add things. Teach him to multiply and divide things. When it comes time for fractions, bake a pie and use it as a model. Show your child the concrete reality of mathematical structure.

I realize that math at its higher level is abstract and theoretical, but at the basic level it simply can't be that way. The child can't handle those abstractions. To present any kind of numbering principle without showing him the concrete reality it represents is not only slow and futile, but it can also be discouraging to the child.

Let me assure you that there is a very real psychological phenomenon called "math block" or "math anxiety." I have seen junior high and high school students so frightened by the prospects of mathematics that their whole system runs amok. I am not sure I know all the reasons, but I suspect one of them is that the child was presented abstract math before his mind was ready for it.

When your child says, "I don't see," he means it literally. The way to teach him is to show him something he can see with his eyes. Show him something concrete.

The principle of instruction is simple and easy to apply. For one thing, children want to count and add and multiply things. Put them to work at it.

Send the child to the pantry for seven potatoes. Have him count the railroad cars. When you have your child help you count the Christmas cards, use a tally system so he will get the idea of a nine-base numbering system. As your child becomes proficient with his counting, show him how to count by twos or threes. Use the same principle in teaching him all of the mathematical operations.

Math Is Fundamental to Intellect

Buying a calculator won't solve problems with math. Basic human intellect requires a working knowledge of math. I admit that adding, subtracting, multiplying, and solving square roots are machinelike functions sometimes performed better by the machine than by our brains. But these are basic intellectual skills. Most of higher learning is based on these principles. If the child fails to master these basic facts, he will always have intellectual limits. Since so much of our knowledge and so much of our intellectual ability is based on these mathematical facts, the child simply must learn them.

Oh, how I wish there were a creative synonym for that last *learn,* but there isn't. Theses are facts, rote facts, and the child has to *learn* them that way; he has to *memorize* them. We can talk about putting a little variety in the activity, and perhaps even camouflaging it so the child won't know he is learning anything, but it is still memorization and drill. Since these facts are learned through drill, they have to be recited often and with immediate feedback.

Consequently, your child's teacher is not going to have enough class time to give your child as much work as he probably needs. If he is ever going to learn his multiplication tables well enough to keep from getting cheated at the checkout counter, you will have to help him drill. It is just another one of those duties of parenthood.

What method you choose for drilling depends on your personality and patience. If you are into the rapid, straightforward approach, you can use the oral method—problems and answers. But that ignores my first principle that it should be concrete. Flash cards help a little, but it would be even better if you had the child add the flash cards rather than compute the problems written on them. However, these methods are fast and portable, and your child may find them entertaining. Drills may be more fun than riding in a car or sitting in the doctor's office with nothing to do.

Some games are excellent. A good, long game of Monopoly might teach your child about as much math as he will cover in a semester, particularly if you make him the banker. If you don't have games or your child doesn't seem to be interested, make up games that interest him. The only rule is that someone has to keep score.

I once watched two second graders play the hand-slap game for about an hour. It is actually rather simple and portable. The person who's "it" holds his hands upside down at waist level. The other person rests his hands on top. "It" jerks one or both of his hands out and slaps the other person's hands before he can move. These two second graders had worked out a point system, so that they were practicing their arithmetic while entertaining themselves on a stalled school bus. Try something like that with your child. It might be fun for the two of you to invent a math-learning game. You can both play enthusiastically.

I also encourage you to give the child some responsibility to use his math skills in a practical way. Of course, you have to adjust the problem to his skill level, but you can give him a feeling of the importance of this information he has been storing in his brain. For example, present questions such as, "I need a gallon of milk at $1.89 and a loaf of bread at 66¢. Will I have enough left out of my $5.00 to buy you that box of crayons?"

That ought to start the brain clicking. With a problem like this, he will not only practice his rote skills of computation, he will also begin to use higher-level problem-solving skills. Use every opportunity you get to engage your child in this kind of activity. When it is convenient, have him solve problems of measurement, time, and percentage. This way, he will become familiar with particular kinds of solutions. Have him figure the baby-sitter's fee. If he is interested in sports, introduce him to the wonderful world of batting averages or field goal percentages.

Math problems are all around us. With just a little imagination, you can bring the real world into your child's learning so that he will not only have the concrete representation, but he can also see the purpose for all that rote drill.

Math Is Not Exclusive to the Male Mentality

I am not trying to get into trouble here; I am trying to avoid it. Statistics tend to indicate that mathematics is a male-dominated field. There are more males than females in the higher-level math courses in high school and college. More men than women enter the math-related fields. (That makes sense, given the first statistic.) But this is a cultural phenomenon rather than a natural one. There is nothing inherent in the study of mathematics that says your ninth-grade daughter should have a natural block against learning algebra. If she has such a block, it was learned and not inherited.

Through the years, I have become convinced that math interest and ability is largely the result of early training and association. For example, at our college a few years ago, we graduated three very fine female math teachers. One was a farmer's daughter who had to count cows and measure the corn when she was young. Another was the daughter of an architect whose home is filled with math games and erector sets. The third was a daughter of a math teacher. I rest my case.

If you don't want your daughter to fall in among the bad attitudes toward math, surround her with the reality of concrete mathematical problems and encourage her as she grows. And that is also good advice when dealing with your son.

Like reading and writing, mathematical operations are learned skills. With the proper stimuli, circumstances, supervision, and encouragement, children can become proficient enough at those skills to achieve their created potential.

Homework Assignments for Parents

1. Do you have any negative attitudes toward math that your child may be picking up on? If so, how can you eliminate them?

2. What concrete illustrations can you come up with to help your child understand whatever mathematical functions he is learning at the moment?

3. How can you make some of the "learn-by-rote" and memorization portions of mathematical learning a little less monotonous for your child?

9

The Fourth 'R': Religion

s your child develops his skills of reading, writing, and mastering mathematics, he will become more aware of himself and his environment. Naturally, he will begin to ask questions about his role in that environment. He may not always know that he is asking those questions, but he is; and such curiosity is spiritual in its character.

I don't intend to anticipate the Holy Spirit here and say that every child automatically pauses somewhere in the middle of the second grade and analyzes his relationship with God. Yet a growing knowledge does lead the child to a need for more answers.

Whether or not your child has made a profession of faith, you must realize his specific needs for instruction and direction during this critical period when his knowledge level is expanding so rapidly. Usually his spoken or subconscious spiritual questions can be classified into three types: knowledge of God and Christ, the nature of faith, and applied values.

In this brief chapter, I will not attempt to anticipate nor to answer all the questions, but only suggest a framework for you to use in understanding what is happening to your child. There are some very intelligent people who have devoted their lives to understanding the spiritual needs of young children. I recommend that you spend some time becoming familiar with their ideas and insights. You can find their books at your local bookstore.

Knowledge of God and Christ

Perhaps the most important thing for you to remember about your child is what you learned in the last chapter—that at this age he is a concrete thinker. He is simply more comfortable thinking about things he can see and hear. The magnificent, eternal, omnipresent character of God may baffle him. In fact, Jean Jacques Rousseau once said that any child who believes in God is an idolater. I think Rousseau was wrong because he underestimated the capacity of children, but we do need to realize their limitations in spiritual understanding.

During this time when the child is beginning to use his mental powers to interpret the written codes of culture, we need to present a God he can know concretely, the God of creation. Observe with him the changing of the seasons, birds flying South in winter, the swallows returning to Capistrano, individual fingerprints, the beauty of a tree, the four-o'clock plant which closes its blossoms in the daytime. All these proclaim coherence, order, and unity. Create devotions from these things and your child will soon begin to see the Mind that has made them.

Since the child is developing his ability to read, now is the time to stimulate his interest in discovering God's Word. If he can't read well enough to handle the actual Scripture, find him a good Bible storybook. If your library doesn't have one, drop into your church library or a Christian bookstore. There are several good books available.

You can also supplement the Bible storybooks with other children's books written from a Christian perspective. Any story that teaches the child the nature and character of God or introduces him to the well-known stories in Scripture is a valuable experience at this stage, particularly if the story is written so the child can read it himself and stay interested in it. Such reading will help build some anticipation for reading the Bible, and it will give him a background for grasping the Scripture when he gets to it.

Through the years, I have talked with several beginning readers who have developed an unhealthy fear of the Bible because of the way it was treated in sermons, Sunday school classes, or even in the home. One of the difficult characteristics about rearing a prereader is that we are never quite sure what they hear and how they interpret what they hear. You can guard against your child's inadvertently developing a fear of Scripture by providing him with exciting devotional reading.

Just recently, I saw the results of a poll of librarians who had named C. S. Lewis's *The Lion, the Witch, and the Wardrobe* as one of the top ten children's books of all times. That is quite a recommendation, particularly from a group that is not necessarily Christian. Again, visit your library or bookstore. There is an ample supply of solid, well-written material the child can read on his own in his search for understanding God and God's place in his life.

At the same time though, don't give him the total responsibility to find out on his own. Now is the time to involve the child actively in family devotions. If your family has not been having regular group devotions, you may want to start during this time when your child is moving from a nonreading into a reading world. The group devotion is probably more important at this point than at any other stage in the child's development.

The child is being introduced to such a variety of topics, issues, and values that he needs some framework for basing his questions so he can handle all that new information. Provide him with that structure. You don't have to be a theologian or a great preacher. Read, pray, and listen to the child's questions and ideas. He will understand if you have to search for answers. But through all this he should get the idea that his spiritual life matters to you and to him.

The Nature of Faith

Christian parents frequently ask me, "At what age is a child old enough to hear and understand the message of salvation so that he can make a profession of faith?" My answer is probably too simple: "When he asks." But I am willing to live with that answer as a general principle.

When your child comes to you with questions that indicate he is concerned about death, heaven, hell, or his own relationship with Christ, he is ready to have those questions answered succinctly and simply. He doesn't need tons of sermons. He doesn't need to study the four spiritual laws. He needs to know that Christ worked out the plan of salvation on the cross and in resurrection. The child also needs to know that he can have a personal relationship with his eternal Savior through faith and prayer.

This may seem like an oversimplification of all the mysteries of theology, but Christ taught us that faith is simple. Let the child understand simply. As he grows intellectually, his understanding will grow. If your child is old enough to ask, he is old enough to believe.

If you don't feel comfortable answering his questions yourself, you may want to seek some outside help; but be careful about whom you choose. This is a special time for your child. These are very personal questions he is asking. Unless your child is particularly bold and outspoken, it probably took a lot of courage just for him to ask you. Help him guard the personal, private character of his search for a meaningful relationship with God. If your child knows the pastor personally, the pastor can help. But if the pastor doesn't know your child, the pastor is a wrong choice. Pick someone who has at least had a conversation with your child before this time.

On occasion, I have been asked to meet with children I don't know. Inevitably, the situation becomes embarrassing for the child, for the parents, and for me. I consider myself fairly effective in talking with children. (Having a twelve-year-old mind is of some advantage.) But I am never good in these sessions. Regardless of my jovial nature, the child simply doesn't know me well enough to share those personal, profound thoughts that have been flashing across his mind. These are things you only share with someone who loves you.

But what if your child never comes to you with the questions, or doesn't even hint that he has considered the questions? How long do you wait for him to make the move? Is there something a parent can do to lead the child toward readiness for faith? Yes, obviously.

After you have provided your child with reading materials, church opportunities, and at least some family devotional sessions, you may want to encourage him to ask his questions by asking some questions of your own. Look for the proper opportunity, sometime when you and your child are feeling good about being related to each other, when you are both happy and honest, and ask him what he thinks about Christ. What does he think are the advantages of being a Christian? What does he think about the value of prayer?

If he is reluctant to talk about those things, answer your questions yourself; then drop the matter. In a few weeks when another opportunity presents itself, come back to the same questions.

There are, however, a couple of notes of caution. Although I realize that the Christian message is victory over death, *be cautious about overemphasizing the death theme with a child of this age.* It is quite possible that this theme could so completely dominate his mind that he loses sight of the real theme of victory.

The early Puritans didn't have any reservations about this. Their children's literature is laced with the idea of death. *The New England Primer*, a popular primary textbook in colonial America, taught children the letter *X* by having them recite this verse: "Xerxes the Great did die, and so must you and I." It also taught the child the letter *F* with: "The idle Fool is whipped at school." I am not convinced that children need to dwell on the idea of death before they are fully prepared to handle the perplexity.

The second note of caution is that you *make sure the climate is right.* Since you are seeking to enter the child's most inner being, don't do it in a moment of anger which would only make the child defensive.

On occasions, both as a parent and a teacher, I have felt like yelling, "You stupid jerk. You are going to hell if you don't change your heart and ways." But that probably isn't the right thing to say, particularly at the moment of anger. Wait for a time when your child is not defensive or trembling. Wait for the moment when both of you can be honest.

Applied Values

I had first planned to make value development a separate chapter, but that wouldn't be in keeping with my ideas of values. I realize that there are values apart from religion. I realize that nonbelievers are capable of building a structure of valuing that can be as specific and novel as mine which flows from a personal commitment to living a God-centered life.

But the difference is that the Christian's value structure has a base. He knows the source of the instruction that directs his beliefs and his behavior. Regardless of situations, his basic commitment cannot change. It just seems appropriate that a discussion of your child's value development should be included in the discussion of his spiritual development.

The first few years in school are critical. For one thing, when the child starts school, he simply doesn't spend as much time with you. He has more opportunity to make his own decisions and act on them. Since he is growing in independence and self-control, he will now confront issues that have never really been an issue before. He has to take charge of at least some areas of his own life.

This first taste of the power of decision-making comes at a time when the child is not very reasonable. He has not yet developed the ability to reason through actions and see the long-range consequences. He has to limit his thoughts to what a decision is going to mean to him at the moment.

At this stage, the key to his value decisions may be acceptance and approval. If he wants to please you and win your approval, he will probably do what he thinks it will take to please you. However, as his social circles broaden, don't be surprised if he decides he would rather win some other person's approval (such as a playmate who encourages him to play with matches or throw snowballs at cars).

As the child grows in independence, moral decisions become more difficult. The difference between right and wrong becomes less clear than it once was.

In order to sort through things, most children try trial and error. They decide (perhaps not consciously) to experiment with behaviors to see how they like them. The problem for the parent is to keep from panicking.

How often a distraught parent has called me with the shameful confession, "My seven year old has lied to me." For some reason, that first lie is a real shocker.

I remember the first time each of my children lied to me. I was heartbroken, beside myself, and I made a vow never to admit it to anyone. Fifteen years later, I am amused at how I responded, not only to the lie but to a lot of experimental behavior during that time when the child was first adjusting to the new social and moral demands of school. If your child is to develop any kind of moral self-control, he has to experiment. You can keep your sanity by telling yourself, *Maybe it won't look all this bad twenty years from now.*

But you can—you must—provide the base and the feedback. Trial and error is not a bad learning technique if the child knows what he should do and when he gets out of line. Be prepared to tell him. Don't confuse your child by reserving your judgment about his behavior. If you are really disturbed, make the message emphatic enough that the child will remember your displeasure the next time he faces the same opportunity. That emphatic message is called punishment, but we will get back to that later.

Make sure your child knows what you value. There are two ways to communicate this—tell him and show him. Use your devotional sessions to teach him what the Bible says about taking care of his body and managing social relationships. When your child is at this stage of intellectual and moral development, you can be matter-of-fact and specific. "I do this because this is what God's Word tells me to do."

I realize that this sounds authoritarian, but at this age the child will respond to authority. Rejoice for now. When he gets to junior high, that approach won't work anymore. He will bug you for the reason behind every decision you or God ever made.

This authoritarian base becomes a benchmark. The child may be disobedient, but at least he knows it. He has to make a choice to disobey.

Without this base, he only confuses himself, and his trial-and-error approach runs on endlessly. Besides, we have the promise of Scripture itself that this kind of instruction will be blessed by God as the child grows.

To show you what kind of an old traditionalist I am, I still believe in having the child memorize some Bible verses. It definitely won't hurt him. Memorizing is good mind skill, and it might be invaluable.

When my child comes to the place where he has to make a decision about using drugs (and almost every child growing up in this country will eventually face that decision), I want him to remember Paul's admonition about his body being a temple of the Holy Spirit. That may not deter my child, but it will make him know that what he is doing is wrong. I want the biblical value structure planted firmly in his mind.

When your child makes a decision to transgress his basic value structure, you need to remind him. How you choose to remind him should depend on what your child needs rather than how angry you are at the moment. In other words, if you have to punish your child, remember *why* you are punishing him.

You are not trying to prove that you are bigger than he is; he knows that already. You are not trying to show that you have been hurt or wronged. You are trying to show your child that he has made an inaccurate moral choice, and you are trying to remind him not to do it again. Effective punishment gets that message across.

You may need to be creative. The standard "belt to the seat" may not always be the best way to convey that idea. Personally, I have always found the most painful punishment for a mistake is to have to make restitution. But whatever punishment or reminder you choose, let the child make full restitution. When the punishment is complete, forget the crime. Go right back to your relationship as if nothing ever happened. The ability to forget and return to normal is not always easy, but it is vital.

As your child develops his intellectual tools of reading, writing, and problem solving, he will also develop a spiritual awareness. And this spiritual awareness comes at a time when his expanding social contacts put him into the position of making significant moral decisions. In an almost contradictory manner, as the child grows in school, his need for solid, parental instruction increases. Children are fun at any age, but they are particularly fun at this age when they need us the most.

Homework Assignments for Parents

1. In what ways are you teaching your child about the nature of God?

2. As your child develops questions concerning faith, are you prepared to discuss such matters with him? Do you have an outside source (or sources) who can help you if necessary?

3. Are you rational and consistent when it comes to punishment as well as in modeling positive values for your child?

4. Do you have family devotions? How would you get them started (or improve existing ones)? In what ways can you get your child more directly involved?

SECTION 3:
TEACHING YOUR CHILD
RESPONSIBILITY

10

The Dependent/ Independent Paradox

"**W**hen I have children of my own, I will never tell them one day that they are too old for irresponsible behavior, then tell them the next day they are too young to be trusted with responsibility."

Do you remember making statements like that when you were young? Oh, well. Being a parent is far more humbling than planning to be one.

But children do get confused as we confront a dependent/independent paradox during that time when the child is first making his adjustment between home and school. It is quite possible that the authorities in his life don't always agree on how much of his own decision-making he is capable of handling at that particular time.

At home he may get the idea that he is still a child, needing constant supervision and protection. At school he may feel that he has a lot of adult responsibility, such as taking care of his own possessions and managing his own time.

Or it may be the other way around. He may get the idea that he is trusted at home, but not trusted at school. Or he may even get the idea that both teachers and parents seem to trust him with some matters of responsibility but don't trust him with others. It may not even occur to the adults that they are projecting ths confusion, but it can be very disconcerting to the average eight year old.

Striving for Consistency

The whole matter deserves some of your time for evaluation. It is not so much a question of asking if you are expecting too much or too little from your child. Rather, it is more a question of whether you and the other authorities in his life are consistent with your expectations.

Do you pin notes on his shirt or expect him to be responsible enough to get the message to the right person? At what age do you allow him to handle telephone messages? Do you check to see if he ate his lunch, or do you leave that to his own choice? How do you send his fees to school? When do you give him a key to the house? At what age is he responsible enough to stay home without a baby-sitter? Do you trust him to do his homework or do you check on him every day? What do you do when he loses something? To what degree is he responsible for the way he looks—clothes, hair, nails?

There are actually two goals to work toward. First, you want to make sure you don't give the child so much independence or responsibility that you frustrate him or drive him to compensate by acting more grown up than he really is. At the same time, you want to give him enough responsibility to challenge him to continue to grow toward becoming a responsible person.

Determining the proper amount of independence or responsibility may be one of the toughest tasks of parenthood. My oldest daughter is twenty-four and has been married for two years, but I am still wondering if she is mature enough to handle her life. Somehow the parental urge to protect gets in the way when we think about giving a child a little room for independence.

Although I don't have any suggestions about how to establish a consistency of expectation toward your child, I do have some suggestions that can help you assist him in growing more independent. And by growing more independent, he is more likely to adjust to the varying levels of expectations.

1. *Give your child some chores.*

If you live on a farm with horses, chickens, cows, and a garden, this is a rather simple suggestion. But if you are a typical suburban parent, chores are a little tougher to find. This may be the biggest challenge of child rearing for the suburban or urban parent. Where are we going to find enough responsible chores to help our children grow into responsible people? Where are we going to find enough significant work to teach our children that the work must be done?

Sometimes we have to look deep and be creative. You may want to buy a family pet to provide some added responsibility! You may need to take a hard look at all those labor-saving devices you have been wanting.

In our town we get somewhere between thirty and a hundred inches of snow a year. For several years I have wanted a snowblower. I can even afford to buy one. But I will not buy one as long as I still have children at home. Shoveling is a family task. We all must assume the responsibility for keeping the walks clean. I have even come to the point where I actually thank God for snow.

Doing chores teaches a child many things. Obviously, it teaches him to handle responsibility and independence. But it also helps him get the message that he is an important person. He is making some contribution to the world. He is worthwhile while he is still growing.

These are important lessons, and they are worth teaching in spite of all the protests you may get from your child. Persist. Demand. Expect. The end result is worth the determination it may take to get there.

2. *Expect your child to do the chores.*

Bear with me. I am about to say something controversial here. I believe it is important that we teach a child to do chores for no other reason than that we expect him to do them. I am not too ecstatic about the practice of paying a child some fee for every little bit of work he performs around the house.

I do understand the need to teach a child the value of work and the idea that money comes from work. But I believe more strongly in teaching the child the importance of necessity: "For now, you do the job because it has to be done. There will be time for those other lessons later and in a different context. You do the job because you are old enough to assume some responsibility for your own being. You do the job because I expect you to do it."

I have heard children ask, "What will you give me if I do it?" It seems to me that is the same question as, "What will happen to me if I don't do it?" I think both are dangerous questions. In the child's mind, the reward or the punishment becomes more important than the responsibility. He is not learning much about independence from this kind of situation.

I have been around children in huge quantities for more than twenty-five years, and the one thing I have come to believe with the greatest conviction is that children usually do what is expected of them. I even have tons of research to support that conviction. If you assign your child a chore and sincerely expect him to do it, he will have learned something about responsibility and independence. You may even be surprised at his capability.

3. *Start your child on some kind of allowance as soon as he is able to count money.*

No! That is not contradictory to the point above. These are two different suggestions. Don't make the allowance circumstantial. He gets the money regardless of whether he does his chores. (We will get to this possibility in the next point.)

The amount of the allowance is not all that important. Don't worry if you can't afford very much (and don't be embarrassed if your child's friend gets twice as much). The important thing here is the lesson, not the money. But give the child the allowance and help him work out a budget (include the tithe and other essentials), and expect him to stick to it. You may be pleasantly surprised at how quickly your child grows into some responsible attitudes.

4. *Make your child responsible for his own actions.*

When he fails to do something he should have done or does something he shouldn't have, handle the situation in such a way that he suffers the consequences of his own action. This is actually more difficult than spontaneous punishment. If he doesn't do his chores, don't spank him or withhold his allowance. That would be too easy! Make him do his chores.

Take the word of experience here. If you wake an eight year old out of a warm bed to carry out the garbage at 1:00 A.M., he probably won't forget next week. Spanking him would have been easier, but it wouldn't have taught him the lesson you wanted him to learn.

There is actually a higher-level suggestion implied in this. Don't punish the *child;* punish the *action.* In other words, when it is possible, make the punishment grow out of the action.

This way, the child will get the idea that you approve of him. You just don't like what he did.

5. *Make your child responsible for his own possessions and environment.*

Occasionally, I hear about some mother who discovers disturbing material while cleaning her child's room. I sympathize with that mother, but I always wonder why she was cleaning the room in the first place. I hope she was just snooping.

As any teacher will tell you, a child old enough to read and write is old enough to keep his own room clean. He may need a little supervision or occasional help, or he may even have to be told when his idea of cleanliness falls below acceptable standards. But the child should be given the bulk of the responsibility for keeping his room clean. As I have said frequently, it might be easier to do it yourself than to persist, but the child needs the joy of being responsible for his own affairs.

This same lesson applies to possessions. Except for such things as clothes, which require special attention, the child needs the responsibility of managing his own property. He must be aware of where things belong, and he needs to be taught to keep his things in order. If he loses something, he should have to find it. You may want to help him with the search, but the primary responsibility for the hunt should be his. If he destroys something, he should suffer the loss.

These are both personal and social rules. In the school setting, your child will be expected to be responsible in such matters. You can help the teacher manage those thirty students by making sure your child is developing a sense of independence while he is adjusting to school during those first three years. As he becomes more independent, he will develop self-control. The next three chapters contain some specific suggestions for helping develop responsibility in your child.

Homework Assignments for Parents

1. Evaluate the level of independence your child has been showing. In what ways is it positive? In what ways is it negative?

2. What new chores can you assign your child to help him become more independent?

3. The next time your child neglects to complete an assigned chore, what can you do to make sure he doesn't get by with dodging his responsibility?

4. How can you help make your child more responsible for his possessions, the appearance of his room, etc.?

11

Letting Go

The sight of tears is not unusual for first-grade teachers, particularly during the early weeks of the year—especially right after lunch. Many children accustomed to half-day kindergartens still have to adjust in order to control their bodies, minds, and emotions for a full day. It is frequently a time for tears.

One teacher planned her day's activities accordingly. After lunch, she spent thirty minutes reading to the children. As they listened, she encouraged them to sit quietly and put their heads down on the desk. That way, no one except her would notice any tears.

When one girl continued to cry long after the usual number of days, the teacher became a bit concerned. The girl appeared cheerful enough during the rest of the day and seemed to enjoy learning. The teacher couldn't understand the problem. So after a while, she approached the little girl and expressed her concern.

"Oh," the girl reported, "I love school, but I am worried about my mother. She is home all day without me and I am sure she is lonely. We had good times together when I was home with her."

As we worry about our children and how they adjust, we also need to realize that they worry about us as well. The way a parent adjusts to a child's new life will have an impact on how the child adjusts.

Growth is always accompanied by mixed emotions. On the one hand, we celebrate and jump for joy to see the changes in our children. On the other hand, in our quieter moments of reflection, we wonder whether either one of us is ready for all that change.

Whenever your child masters a new skill, he also achieves a new level of independence. When he learns to tie his own shoes, he simply doesn't need you as much as he once did. Those special moments when you tied his shoes and then hugged him for good measure (just because you had him close enough) are gone forever. Now you will have to find another excuse to get close to him, and there may not be as many hugs as there were before!

Sure, I want my child to grow. I like to brag about his accomplishments. I like to show him off when company comes. I like to feel good about his progress. But I must admit that it is painful to turn him loose and give him the freedom and independence he needs in order to grow. Let's think about some reasons for this ambivalence.

Fear of the Child's Failure

Any parent who has watched a child learn to walk wishes there were some guaranteed method for controlling the learning laboratory, so the child would experience only painless falls. But there is no such method. Both the child and the parent have to take some risks. In every aspect of human growth, there is always some implied risk and usually some failure.

When parents send their children to that other learning laboratory called school, they probably would like the same kind of guarantee they wanted when the children learned to walk—that there won't be any painful falls, hurts, or failures. But no such guarantee is provided. In spite of the best advice given by all of us who claim to know something about schools and children in schools, and in spite of all your concern and direction as a parent, there just isn't any guarantee that your child will adjust to school, learn to read, develop a whole stable of new friends, and become popular and successful without some trying and painful moments.

So how do you know if he is ready? What are you going to do to help him? Wouldn't it just be easier to protect him from all the possibilities of hurt? Probably, but then there wouldn't be any growth. So you may as well prepare yourself for the ordeal of allowing your child some room to fail. Here are a few things to keep in mind.

1. *Failure is time-consuming.*

Often it would just be quicker to do something yourself than to deal with the mess your child is going to make while he is learning. Maybe you would really like to introduce your six year old to the nightly ritual of doing the dishes. But that means that you would have to teach him how first, and that you would have to go through it with him a couple of times. Then you would have to turn him loose to do the job by himself a couple of times, and then go in to rewash, redry, and rearrange whatever he goofed up.

It might save you a lot of time in the long run for him to master that skill, but right now you really don't have time to let him do it wrong enough times to learn how to do it right. It is just easier to do it yourself.

2. *Failure is emotionally consuming.*

When your child gets hurt physically or emotionally, you have to stop what you are doing to patch him up. That not only takes time, but it also wears you both out. No caring parent can be happy when he knows his child is hurting, so during the period following failure you have to work especially hard at understanding the full complexity of your child.

A happy child is a rather simple little being. He carries his happiness and his reasons for happiness right out in front so everyone can see them. But a sad child, a hurting child, a child despondent over a sense of failure is complex. The parental task of applying the soothing salve to the hurt is compounded because of those complexities.

Why is he hurt? Why does he respond that way when he is hurt? What is the damage of that failure? How quickly should I "persuade" (force) him to tackle that challenge again? When he almost drowns, how quickly do I put him back into the pool? What can I do to help him forget or accept his failure? Should I leave everything alone and let him grow through the experience?

These are tough questions, and the pursuit of answers is an emotionally consuming chase. My life as a parent would be simpler if both the child and I could forget about having him take the risks necessary to grow. Oh, the pains of letting go!

3. *Failure often requires parents to think like children.*

For us to understand failure, we have to look at the undertaking through the children's eyes. We have to define success in their terms and not ours, which isn't easy.

I was visiting a young father when his seven-year-old daughter and her friend came in, dragging some old, rotten boards they had dug out of a neighbor's trash.

"May we borrow your saw?" the daughter asked.

"What for?"

"We're going to make a dollhouse," she announced.

"Well, why don't you wait until I am finished, and I'll get you some better boards. I will help you, and we will make a good-looking dollhouse," the father offered.

It was clear that his suggestion didn't please either of the young girls. They went back outside to play and soon forgot their urge to build a dollhouse.

Obviously, the two parties were at cross-purposes. The father was seeing the prospect of a product, and anything that fell short of his idea of the product would have been a failure. On the other hand, the girls were seeing the prospect of the *process*. They really didn't care what the dollhouse looked like. The fun and the success were in the making, not in having a finished *product*. Any dollhouse would have met their standards, so long as they had built it themselves.

To understand failure and success, sometimes parents have to think like children. That may be one of the hardest tasks of giving the child enough freedom to experiment. Although you may be convinced that he can make his printed letters better, they might have looked rather good to him. He might really have been satisfied with the task until you told him he had failed.

Nevertheless, failure is definitely a part of growing, and if our children are going to grow, we are going to have to give them the freedom and the support to fail.

Regrets and Resistance

Most parents, when pressed to the wall, will admit that we like people at one age better than we like them at another. Notice, I didn't say anything about love. Parental love is a constant. You will always love your child regardless of what hideous stage he may be going through at the moment. But there will be times when you won't like him as much as you do at other times.

I think many of us like little children—their spontaneous shows of affection, the honesty, the innocence, the loyalty, the attention they give to us as parents because of their inability to fulfill their own needs. And somehow we know that as the child grows in size and capabilities, some of those qualities will be lost. Since we can't predict what the child is going to be like in the future, we tend to cling to him the way he is now. We like him this way. We would just as soon keep him this way as long as we can.

A child's growth potential demands some faith on our part. We have to turn loose of the person we know and love, and we have to trust God for the unknown person he is going to become.

Sometimes we are afraid to give the child room to grow because we don't want to admit that we are growing into another stage of life. I didn't recognize this as a problem until the last of our three children reached school age. One day Mary and I both awoke to the sobering fact that we were out of babies. That part of our lives was over. We just didn't feel at home in toy stores anymore. Just about the time I got really good at doing distinctive voices for each of the three bears, my audience learned to read and didn't need my help. We even got kicked out of the young parents' class at Sunday school. Middle age became a reality all too soon.

We responded to that awful truth with dignity; we tried to keep our last child a baby much longer than we had the others. We just didn't turn loose. We didn't welcome her growth with as much celebration as we should have. We didn't give her as much independence. We tried as long as we could to avoid the reality of our own need to grow. Finally, we gave in. We had to. She got her own job, her own driver's license, and her own set of friends, activities, and aspirations. So now we sit in Sunday school with all those middle-aged folks and tell ourselves that we really don't look that old.

Regardless of the thrill that comes when your child loses a tooth or learns to ride a bike, there still may be something in you that protests the process in progress. That is fairly normal. But you have to deal honestly with those feelings, and someday you will have to turn your child loose.

Homework Assignments for Parents

1. Do you ever allow your child to fail, or do you do everything you can to have him avoid that process?

2. How do you respond to your child's failures? (Think of some specific illustrations before you answer.)

3. Think of some recent examples of times you let your child go in order for him to grow. Also recall some times when you might have held on too long. In retrospect, would you change the way you handled any of those situations?

4. What effect, if any, has your child's entering school had on the morale of you and your spouse?

12

Outside Activities

When your child starts school, your family is soon faced with another big decision. How involved is he going to be in activities outside the home and the school? This is a question the whole family must answer, because the child's participation will require some kind of commitment from all family members. It directs time schedules, causes transportation problems, and requires your active encouragement and perhaps instruction in another phase of growth. So you had better decide at the onset: is the activity worth the effort?

To answer this, you need to assess the actual value of the participation to both the child and the family. To facilitate your evaluation, we can classify these outside activities into three groups: participation activities, instructional activities, and clubs.

Participation Activities

In this category, I include organized sports teams as well as music and drama groups. Although there is some instruction inherent in the very nature of these activities, the groups are primarily for the purpose of giving the child the social structure for participation.

The directing principle determining your child's involvement is an honest answer to a simple question: *Why do you want your child to participate?* Does he have the desire? Do you think it will be educational? Or are you interested in fulfilling some of your own aspirations through your child?

Some six-, seven-, and eight-year-old children are mature enough to handle the new experiences that an orchestra or sports team will provide. Others aren't. There is nothing sadder than to watch a seven year olds' baseball game where four mature athletes dominate the contest at the expense of all players involved.

If your child really wants to join a sports team (baseball, football, soccer, wrestling, and hockey seem to be the most popular), I wouldn't propose to take this experience away from him. But I see no need to force a child into such an experience when he is neither physically nor emotionally mature enough to enjoy some success. If your child is interested, he may be ready.

On the other hand, if you have great visions of being the parent of the world's first eight-year-old all-American quarterback, you need to look somewhere else to fulfill your fantasies. Being eight years old is tough enough in itself. Your child doesn't need the added burden of carrying you on his back.

Don't force your child into any activity in which he has to adopt your standard of success. That is unfair to the child. If he does choose to play, help him set realistic standards for himself. Even the pros occasionally boot a ground ball or blow a wrong note.

If your child is talented and mature enough to master the skill of the activity, the whole experience can be quite educational for him. He can learn how to function in a group and to deal with success and failure. Through participation he will surely develop his skills in the activity. But the question is at what age we need to start him so that he will learn the valuable lessons without first deciding that he doesn't like the activity.

Frequently I meet parents who tell me that they suspect their child is talented. They don't want to cheat him out of the opportunity to be as good as he can be. I agree with them. We should give our children every chance to achieve their created potential. But as a college football coach, I am convinced that it is not necessary to start a child into sports before his body and emotions are mature enough to handle the rigors and discipline of the sport.

We have fine college players who never participated in organized sports, much less football, until they were in high school. We even have a few players who started football after they were in college. Usually these young men bring a refreshing eagerness to the game which the early starters have lost somewhere in the many seasons they have played.

My music consultants tell me the same is true with band and orchestra. Enthusiasm for practice and playing is more important than early experience.

Of course, the greatest value of participation is that your child will get the exercise and socialization he needs; so if you and he choose not to participate, you will have to provide him with some other opportunity to keep his body active.

If your child does participate in such organized events, he will still need a great deal of attention and supervision, so your role is just beginning. For one thing, he will need individual instruction and practice in the activity. Playing a horn or throwing a baseball is a physical skill. To master it, your child will have to practice it. If he has any ability at all, the more he practices, the better he will get.

But practice in the individual skills is a one-on-one activity. Just as the teacher does not have enough time to give your child's reading as much attention as it needs, the coach is not going to have enough time to teach him how to catch or throw a baseball.

If you want him to become proficient at these skills, you have to play catch with him. Hour by hour you have to play catch with him. If you agree to let your child participate in organized baseball, it is only fair that you take on this responsibility of helping him develop his skills. It simply isn't fair to let him be embarrassed after the game starts.

You will need to help the child manage the authorities such as the orchestra leader or the coach. Sometimes the people supervising these activities are quite effective at what they do, but some know more about the activity than they know about children. In all my years in sports, the worst tirades and the most unreasonable demands I have ever heard have come not from pro, college, or high school coaches, but from coaches in youth programs. If your child draws one of the sensitive, effective coaches or directors, rejoice. If he gets one of the other kind, consider again why the child is in the activity.

As one final caution, I will say frankly that I am opposed to any activity which alters a child's natural growth in the interest of his sports success. If a boy is active and is eating a balanced diet, I am opposed to his starving some weight off just to participate on the wrestling team. I am opposed to putting him on a weight-lifting program just to pump up his muscles for a football season. Those are activities for adults who have already settled into a body type. Developing children need room to grow naturally.

If you do decide that your child should participate in either a sports, music, or drama program and you don't know where to find one, contact the school. Frequently these programs identify, at least loosely, with the school. If the school people can't help you, try your local community newspapers.

Of course, if you and your child do choose for him to participate in an organized program, you will need to adjust the family schedule to accommodate his commitment. But you know that already, so we will get on to the next kind of activity.

Instructional Activities

Some parents and children choose programs in which instruction is the primary objective. These include such things as dance classes, gymnastic classes, music lessons, or swimming lessons. If you do a bit of research and select the right school, it is possible that your child will get excellent instruction from qualified instructors who understand both the activity and children. Because the supervisor is not responsible for so many children and because the public performance is not as important as in the participation activities, your child should get more individual attention and supervision. Although your child may miss the lessons of teamwork those other activities provide, he will receive more actual instruction and practice in the skill itself.

If your child shows an interest and an aptitude for one of these instructional activities and you are prepared to make the time and financial commitment to it, I would encourage you to choose the school as carefully as you choose a doctor.

Get personal testimony from satisfied customers. Any parent who has been paying for piano lessons will take a few minutes to give you an impression of the teacher.

Check out the facilities. If you choose an activity such as gymnastics which demands huge space and a large investment for equipment, don't be so critical of the actual structure. Look for such things as safety and cleanliness.

Meet the instructors. I repeat myself. Meet the instructors. And soon after your child has started the activity, drop in unexpectedly to watch the lesson in progress.

To you, these lessons represent an investment of time, money, and your own flesh and blood. You are entitled to see what you are paying for. The key to any learning situation is the instructor. A creative instructor who can relate to your child is far more important than the equipment and the facilities.

Another advantage of these schools or classes is that the instructors are usually professional enough to recognize special talent. If your child is particularly gifted, the instructor may be able to spot that talent early, and the school may be able to offer you some advice about how to nurture your child's skill. Remember, however, that children do change in body style and attitude as they develop. If your child shows unusual ability for his age, encourage him, but you both should be prepared for the possibility that his teammates may catch up in a few years.

Of course, these instructional activities do require a financial commitment, so you will always have to consider the cost against the gain. Sometimes such programs might not be feasible regardless of your economic status. But at other times such programs may be so valuable that you will feel like borrowing the money to keep your child involved.

Clubs

On the other hand, the cost of club participation is quite minimal. Such programs as Scouts, Y programs, or church clubs such as Awana, Brigade, Pioneer Girls, G.A., or R.A. offer children a variety of activities at a very low cost.

Although these clubs don't usually offer highly competitive games, the programs are varied enough to satisfy most interests. The meeting usually includes some time for games, crafts, memory work, reading, singing, and special skills. At the same time, each of these clubs is based on the noble purpose of teaching the child some desirable virtues. Although the club may not always be successful, at least the purpose is clear. Your child will be encouraged to join in noble activities.

Another good thing about these clubs is that they offer the child as much or as little participation as he and the family want. If your child wants a casual relationship with Scouts, he can have a casual relationship. On the other hand, if he wants to throw himself into the scouting program, it can consume all of his free time. Although the immediate supervisors may not totally understand this, and they may try to make you feel guilty for less than complete involvement, the program is still there to provide you and your child with what you want and need from it. Don't be afraid to pick and choose.

Since these clubs are usually identified with a specific school or church, you won't have any trouble finding one. Which club you and your child select is a matter of interest. Although each club has a slightly different emphasis, they all begin with a noble purpose and offer an abundance of reasonable activities and services.

Obviously, your primary-age child has a wide assortment of choices for participation in outside activities. In fact, many of these organizations actively recruit, so it would be quite easy for him to develop such a schedule that he could disrupt the family activities every night of the week.

In this case, you and your child may need to learn the meaning of a new word—no. He just can't join everything. He has to make some choices.

It is important for both of you to remember that these outside organizations are designed to supplement the family and even school activities. When they begin to dominate the family schedule, your child is too involved.

With the proper emphasis, participation in these outside activities can be immensely educational, giving your child an opportunity to practice his new sense of independence and social skills and giving him some direction for use of his free time and talent. But I am old fashioned enough to believe that responsibility to family comes first.

Homework Assignments for Parents

1. Do you suspect that your child might have some natural interests in a certain area (or areas)? If so, which one(s)?

2. What things are you doing to ensure that your child is exposed to a number of outside activities from which he can decide what he likes most?

3. Do you think your child is more geared toward participation activities, instructional activities, or clubs? What makes you think so? How can you be sure?

13

At Home Alone

Social scientists frequently invent strange names for human behavior. One of the recent additions to the list is the term *latchkey kids* to designate those school-age children who either come home from school to an empty house or leave in the morning after the adults have already gone to work.

Most of the publicity the term has created has usually leaned toward the negative. Magazine and newspaper articles and radio and television reports not only give us the statistics of the huge number of children who are actually latchkey kids, but they also point out all the possible dangers involved with this activity. Since the practice is so widespread, the issue deserves some attention here, even with parents who are at home when the children get back from school.

Obviously, the topic is deeper than mere statistics and frightening warnings. First, I am not sure I am qualified to question a parent's motive for leaving a child in an empty house. You know your situation and you are the one with the responsibility of making decisions that are most beneficial to all family members. But if you are considering a latchkey situation for your child, either before school or after school, you need to examine the possibility from at least two dimensions—safety and social relationships.

The Safety Element

Since I am writing about first, second, and third graders, my greatest concern is safety. I suspect I have some mother-hen tendencies, but I seem to want all my chicks clustered under the safety of my wing all the time. This safety and age question keeps showing its ugly head throughout child rearing.

When is he old enough to cross the street? When is he mature enough to stay home alone without a baby-sitter? When do we buy him a bicycle and spread his energy over the whole neighborhood? When do we trust him with the car? Do we insist on curfews? And the question at hand: When do I let him come home from school to an empty house?

Of course, the answer to that question depends on several factors—some you can control and some you can't. You have to consider the quality of the neighborhood, the maturity level of the child, the energy of the child, the proximity of neighbors, and your own feelings.

After you have considered all these factors and decided that your child is mature enough to assume responsibility for his own unsupervised care for a part of the day, you need to take charge of those factors you can control. You need to ensure that you have provided some basic elements of safety. Let me suggest some of these.

1. *Teach your child to use the telephone.*

Your child should be told how to use the phone whether he is going to be home alone or not. I am sure you have heard about all the proper techniques the child should use to keep from giving too much information to the wrong party. Make sure he knows not to tell anyone that he is home alone. Make sure he knows how to take a message. Make sure he knows how to guard information about himself.

You need to do more than *tell* this information to your child. Now is the time to *teach* him. Teach him how to respond, then practice with him.

Let him pick up the receiver and talk to you as if you were a stranger calling the house. Make up several different stories and see how the child handles himself. Try to get him confused or flustered. This may seem cruel while you are doing it, but this kind of roleplaying can pay off.

Make sure your child knows how to dial either your work phone or a nearby neighbor. Remember to have him practice this every once in a while so the number is automatic for him. If you want to go further, you may want to make sure he knows the numbers of the fire department and police. Or if you are always available at your work phone, you may choose to have these calls come to you.

2. Prepare the child's after-school snack before you leave the house.

I suspect everybody, teachers and students alike, needs that after-school snack, but fire is one of the biggest safety risks with children in the home. Minimize that bad combination of hunger and risk by having the child's snack prepared so he won't have to turn on any cooking equipment.

3. Plan fire escape routes in your home and practice them occasionally.

Make sure your whole family is prepared for a fire emergency. The preparation doesn't take long, and it can be turned into a fun family experience. We always hope we never have to use such information, but we need to practice just in case.

4. Make sure there is a neighbor close by who can help your child if needed.

Many people in the neighborhood will be glad to keep an eye on your home and to be available in case of an emergency. Again, be sure your child has the appropriate phone numbers memorized.

5. Give the child some chores to do while he is waiting for you to get home.

I realize that it would be much simpler just to have him perch in front of the TV and sit there in a stupor until you get home. But chores will help the time pass faster and will encourage the child to feel that everyone in the family has some of the family responsibility. This way, he will probably assume his role with more maturity.

6. *If you have more than one child at home, make sure you have a good working relationship with the one you leave in charge.*

You have put a big burden of responsibility on that child. Make sure he knows he can talk with you. Make sure you know his thoughts and feelings. If he is missing some of his own childhood activities such as after-school clubs or sports to take care of other children at home, make sure you provide him with ample opportunities to make up what he has missed. Although some children assume the weighty responsibility of the family baby-sitter role at a very young age, they will still need some time to be children without all that responsibility. Help your leader!

From my list, you can begin to formulate your own ideas based on your specific circumstances. If you are going to leave a child at home alone for part of the day, your first task is to do everything possible to provide for his safety. It still won't be as if you were there, but you can minimize the possible dangers.

The Social Element

This leads us to the social relationship dimension, though I am not as concerned about this as I am about the safety considerations.

Leaving your child at home alone for part of the day probably won't do much to alter the family situation if you are a sensitive, caring parent. You can still have a solid, happy family life after you get home. There is still time for praising, hugging, reading, affirming, and all those other activities that make family life special to both children and parents.

The problem here is not the child at home alone, but rather what you value after you do get home from work. If you rush to your own chores and continue to isolate your child, then the family time is going to get out of whack. But you can control this by just making sure you understand what is most important.

In fact, this is one reason why I recommend chores instead of television as a baby-sitter. Since the child has helped you accomplish some of your work, he now deserves some of your attention.

Although the research is rather sparse here, the available material tends to support me. A few years ago, a limited study indicated that children with at least one parent at home through the day got into more school problems than those with working parents. Of course, this isn't a definitive position, but it does indicate that you can make family life significant for your child even though he has to spend some time at home alone.

As a final word, let me remind you that your child needs to know how to get in touch with you at all times. Every principal has horror stories about this.

My most persuasive story is about a young man who fell and broke his arm during basketball class—a compound fracture just above the wrist. After a hurried trip to the hospital, that young man and I waited in the emergency room for three hours while the police tried to track down his mother who was on a neighborhood visiting spree. While I regaled him with every funny story I had ever heard, that brave fellow waited three hours without so much as a painkiller.

That day I vowed to urge all parents to make sure their children can find them in case of an emergency.

Homework Assignments for Parents

1. Don't rule this chapter out just because you don't have a latchkey child. In what instances is your child left alone—even for short periods of time?

2. Out of all of this chapter's suggestions to help your child cope when he is alone, which one(s) are you doing best? Which one(s) do you think you need to work on most?

3. If your child is alone for long periods of time, in what ways do you make it up to him?

SECTION 4: SUPPORT ON THE HOME FRONT

14

The Growth Marks of Success

ast summer, my wife and I painted the living room. In other words, Mary painted and I offered daily critiques. One of the most difficult parts of the job was deciding what to do with that special door frame. You know the one—the door frame where each year for the last ten years we lined the kid up on his birthday, put a straight edge across his head, and recorded his height with a bold pencil mark.

To an outsider, those pencil marks might have looked like any other smudges. But to us, they were significant. They recorded growth—the progress in each child's drive toward becoming an adult. And those smudgy marks did more than record changes in physical growth. They were symbols of changes in attitude, awareness, capability, and independence. Oh, we wiped away a lot of memories with one stroke of a paint brush.

All children have a number of "growth marks," whether or not the marks are noted on a family door frame. And by no means are all growth marks in regard to physical features.

As adolescents or even adults, we occasionally back out of a new task or experience by saying, "I've never done this before." But imagine how many times a child between the ages of six and eight will do something he has never done before. In these three years, your child is going to master for the first time a whole bundle of skills that will become lifetime tools. His growth can be observed and recorded as he moves through these physical, intellectual, and social accomplishments.

Just think of some of the things you can expect your primary child to do for the first time in his life:

- Ride a bicycle
- Tie his shoes
- Use his own house key
- Write his name
- Count to one hundred
- Read a book
- Sleep over at a friend's house
- Tell time
- Make his bed
- Get a new tooth
- Go on a field trip

Children will naturally reach these growth marks at different ages. But the point to remember is that during the next three years, your child is going to achieve a number of first-time accomplishments. These accomplishments provide him with a means for understanding himself and building a healthy self-respect.

To a sophisticated adult, tying a shoe may not seem like a very big deal. To a child, however, the event could have an enormous psychological effect. That small (yet significant) accomplishment could help him realize that as a child of God, he is a capable human being. Such a realization will help him develop a positive self-image, and that self-image will enable him to continue to grow and learn. He is making progress in this journey through life.

Timing Natural Growth

The other day, I asked the expert down the street when I should pick my apples. He said, "When they are ripe." I was never so embarrassed in my life. After all, I say the same thing to parents. If I am asked, "When should I expect our child to achieve this or that?" I answer, "When he is ready."

Intelligence or native ability is one thing, but maturity is something else. Not all children mature at the same time. Some children are ready for new experiences earlier than others.

Just because one child is a little earlier in developing than another doesn't mean that he is brighter, more gifted, or more intelligent. It doesn't mean he has smarter parents or nicer grandmothers. It just means he is maturing a little quicker at this stage of his development.

If your child is a little slower, it isn't anything to be ashamed of. Just stay out of those conversations that make you feel guilty. On the other hand, if your child is one of the quicker ones, enjoy it. He may not always be the earliest maturing child on the block or in the family. Child development is a little fickle that way. The natural development in childhood is not always scheduled to accommodate parents' wishes or expectations.

We must recognize the child's right to develop on the schedule God has ordained for him. I propose that we don't panic just because the child develops a little more slowly in some area than another child. There is a difference between maturity and ability, and we shouldn't confuse the two.

If I could convince you of this one point, first-, second-, and third-grade teachers all over the world would nominate me for the Nobel Peace Prize. The unfortunate custom that puts all children in the first grade at six years of age sometimes makes a mockery out of the Creator's genius in making each of us special. Most are probably ready for the experience and can progress rather well. But some children simply aren't mature enough physically to handle the mechanics of first-grade learning.

When one puts his life into a fifty- or seventy-year perspective, starting school at six or seven is not really that big a deal. As parents, we must make decisions not for the moment and not for the month, but for a whole life span. And to make intelligent decisions, we must recognize each child's special maturity schedule.

Now that I have convinced you of that point, let me say something that may sound almost contradictory. When it comes to timing the growth marks, we don't force a child into a specific growth task until he is mature enough to be ready for the task, but there are some ways to move him toward readiness.

Actually, readiness consists of two dimensions. First, the child has to be physically and emotionally capable of learning and mastering the particular growth mark. And second, the child has to be interested enough to master the task.

Without a ton of sophisticated testing equipment, deciding when a child is physically and emotionally ready is just a matter of judgment. You have studied the child. You have watched him develop. You have worked with him in developing physical skills by playing physical games with him. Through the same games, you have taught him to have the patience it takes to learn by trial and error. Now he is ready to try on his own.

On the other hand, interest can be cultivated. By subtle planning, you might be able to move a child to a position of being interested enough to master the growth mark. Of course, to do this, we need to understand why people are interested in what they are interested in.

Where Does Interest Come From?

Educators usually line up on one of two sides in that debate. Some claim interest is a natural thing that springs spontaneously from the child's sense of pleasure and success. Others claim that interest is the result of hard work. If you work at a job long enough, you will get good at it. Once you develop a little competence, you will learn to like it.

Since you have a child at the stage when he is acquiring new skills and habits, you really need to take a few minutes to ponder this question of interest. What do you do? Do you go ahead and buy that violin, and then force your six year old to stand in front of a music stand for thirty minutes a day producing hideous sounds until he finally learns to make music and love the music he makes? Or do you wait until he comes crawling to you on his hands and knees, begging you for some outlet for his vast musical talents and interests?

Dare we propose a compromise? Perhaps interest is actually the product of imitation. The child sees you do it, and he decides he would like to try. The child decides he would like to read because he sees you reading and enjoying the activity. The child decides he wants to learn to tie a tie because you buy him one. The child wants to learn to play baseball after you take him to a baseball game.

Role modeling is a good teaching technique and imitation is good learning, but teaching through role modeling puts an interesting challenge on the teacher. If you want to promote your child's interest in learning something, you must make sure that what you do is what you want him to imitate.

Timing of many of the growth marks falls into the domain of the school experience. When they fit right into the regular schedule, the child will develop the interest and readiness in the company of his friends and teacher.

Of course, if your child is not making normal school progress in mastering these growth marks (if he is going too fast or too slow), you should find out why. Get the teacher's opinion and match that against yours. If both of you agree that this is a maturity problem, you'll just have to be patient and learn the art of encouraging your child. He is going to need some cheering up when he sees his peers achieve something he hasn't mastered yet.

However, if you suspect something other than a maturity problem, you may want to seek some special help. There are specialists in almost every area of child development, and some of them seem almost to work miracles. (I have seen speech problems completely eliminated in two visits to the therapist.)

But in the midst of all this, the key is not to panic, to keep everything in perspective of a whole life span, and to know your child well enough that you can judge his growth without comparing him with other children.

Celebrate Achievements!

If you ever saw me you might think I was lying, but I have run a marathon. No fooling—26 miles, 385 yards, and a couple of extra inches thrown in for good measure. The day I staggered across that finish line, I didn't need praise. I didn't need to spend any time wondering if the words of the people congratulating me were sincere. At that moment, I was aware of what I was capable of doing with what God had given me. I was aware that, as a creation of God, I probably had more potential than I will ever realize. And in this context, the event gave me purpose and dedication.

To some extent, being able to do a task is reward in itself. When your child conquers something new, you may catch him practicing it over and over. In fact, he may make a nuisance of himself, bothering you for any opportunity to perform his newly acquired growth mark. But it is also important for you as parents to see that such accomplishments are recorded, remembered, and perfected.

How you celebrate these growth mark achievements depends on your family rituals for recognizing such events, but in your celebration you should accomplish three goals:

1. Make sure your child realizes that you think the event is a special accomplishment.

2. Make the child's accomplishment a family affair, so that he will be interested in sharing both his successes and failures in the family setting.

3. Give the moment enough attention that the child will carry the memory of the circumstances and details with him the rest of his life.

During this time when your child is crossing so many new thresholds, it is important for you to remember the significance of each of these events. These are lifetime accomplishments. They are major moments for the child and should be treated as such.

It all passes so quickly. Soon the age of newness and frequent growth marks will be painted over, and that once-helpless child will have achieved a level of independence. As you turn loose of him so that he can grow, and as you help him move toward independence and self-control, make sure you are both developing a catalog of memories so you won't forget what you both learned during this time of rapid growth.

Homework Assignments for Parents

1. What growth marks has your child recently accomplished for the first time?

2. Do you think your child is maturing quicker than most others, slower, or about the same? What are you doing to help him cope with his rate of growth?

3. In what things does your child show special interest at this point in his life? How can you keep him excited and involved in his special interests?

4. In what ways do you usually celebrate your child's achievements?

15

Fostering Creativity

I was jogging on a late February day. The world around me was experiencing an early thaw after a long hard winter. As I dodged the slush and hopped around drifts, I encountered several of the local school children on the way home. One second grader had found a massive icicle, a beautiful piece of natural artwork. It was almost too big for him. But since it was a warm day and he was carrying it cradled in his arms, the icicle was getting smaller every minute.

But the boy still took the time to stop and tell me (and anyone else who would listen) about the wonder of his find. It was the world's largest, he thought. He was going to give it to his mother because she would appreciate it also. He showed us how it was formed drip by drip. And he showed us the beautiful rainbow that glistened so brilliantly when the sun struck it just right. It was such a beautiful icicle and he was so proud of it. I was sorry that it would disappear so soon.

Now I have some idea of what Jesus might have meant when He said that we must become like little children. That afternoon, instead of slush and six-week-old dirty snow, my attention was drawn to the marvelous work of the Creator because I saw it through the eyes of a child.

Creativity Begins at Home

In Chapter 4, we discussed how schools cannot help but encourage conformity. At the same time, parents and teachers agree that creativity is a desirable trait and should be encouraged. In this chapter we want to deal with ways a parent can encourage creativity at home. First, let's review some characteristics of creativity.

Creativity demands time for reflection and trial and error. Creativity begins with what you already know. It's important to have enough time to consider and reconsider your base of information, and then experiment to see how those facts can be put together in new and different ways.

Creativity grows out of confidence. When I am feeling insecure and unloved, I try to do what I think other people expect me to do. I try to win acceptance by conforming. But when I feel good about myself, I can be experimental; I can be creative. For instance, when I feel confident about my knowledge of the English language, then I can be creative with some of the rules.

Creativity can demonstrate itself in many ways. The end product can be as unique as your child. Creativity may be displayed through a poem, a picture, a song, new rules for a game, a birdhouse, a model city, or a new way of coming down the stairs. All these are creative ventures.

Frequently, creative activity is its own purpose. No tangible end product is necessary to show that your child has been creative. Most of the time, the things we do as adults have a desired end result. But creative activity may be its own end. If we are to encourage children to be creative, we must understand their standards.

Let me suggest some things that you can do to help your child see the joy in being inventive.

1. *Encourage him.*

Giving proper encouragement is a challenge. Sure, you are prepared to reward your child when he achieves a school milestone like making a good grade in reading, counting to 100, or writing his name in cursive. But his teachers praise him for those things as well.

It's up to you to encourage him when he does something outside that measured realm. And don't wait around until he constructs some fabulous piece of art. Recognize his uniqueness in the creative thought.

2. *Set some standards for your evaluations.*

Don't overdo your praise regarding your child's creative efforts. He is aware that not everything he does deserves special notice. So before you hang his latest "masterpiece" on the refrigerator door, make sure *he* is happy with it.

3. *Play games that expand his imagination.*

You don't even have to be a creative person to come up with some creative games. Charades is always good because it requires the child to communicate without using words.

Another good game is brainstorming. Hold up some object and have everybody in the room think of unusual ways the object could be used. For practice, let's try a common household sponge. Quickly now, how could we use that sponge? (To drink up the medicine when Mother isn't looking, to hush a certain commentator during the football game, to carry in your pocket so you think you have a wallet full of money when you really don't, to frost and serve as a cake for a practical joke.) Now, you've got the idea. See how easy it is to help your child maintain his creative bent?

4. *Do things that will stimulate your child's senses.*

Just as the game of charades throws your child back on his own initiative by removing his most common means of communication, you can stimulate some of his less-used senses by taking away some of the more active ones. For example, blindfold your child and take him for a walk outside. This will stimulate his senses of touch, hearing, and smell. After you are finished, talk with him about what he remembers.

If you haven't done this, try it yourself. It is rather delightful to become acutely sensitive to the gentle breeze blowing against your face or hear a traffic light changing colors.

While your child is blindfolded, have him identify a whole assortment of things by touch or by smell. When the blindfold is removed, mouth words but don't make any sound. Thus, he will have to read your lips and hear by watching. For the same practice, teach him to mouth words along with his records.

5. *Encourage him to be creative in play.*

I don't want to sound like an old grouch always championing "the good old days," but we don't always do our children great favors by overloading them with toys which leave absolutely nothing to the imagination. I still think that a doll who drinks imaginary milk from a make-believe bottle is more fun than one who drinks real liquid from a real bottle; but you may have to teach your daughter the joys of the imagination!

Creativity is an active process. Some toys make our children too passive in play. Provide simple instruments that your child can transform into sophisticated play equipment by his own imagination.

6. *Create with your child.*

Start a story and let your child come up with an ending. Read a description of a scene, then both of you draw a picture of it. If you suspect he has musical ability (or if you *want* him to have musical ability), play a record and let him lead the imaginative orchestra. Draw pictures together. Write stories together. Show him that you still have an imagination despite all your years in school.

7. *Help him see the creative side of schoolwork.*

Show your child how reading can lead into a world of fantasy. Play some fun arithmetic games. Let me give you an example. You probably learned this somewhere, but let me remind you of the process of "casting out nines" to prove your computation.

44	(add 4+4) =	8
+32	(add 3+2) =	5
76		13
(7 + 6 = 13) (1 + 3 = 4)		(1 + 3 = 4)

Since the two fours match, the problem is correct. (In other words, just keep adding digits until you get into single digits.) Now, try that with subtraction or multiplication. Isn't this fun? Think of the creative person who discovered this little activity. Arithmetic isn't all drudgery.

8. *Provide opportunities for your child to be in creative situations with other children.*

Encourage your child to be in the church play. If he wants to join the orchestra, give him the opportunity. And keep your eyes open for any other group settings of creative young people.

Of course, this list isn't complete, but it can get you started. From here you can use your own inventiveness to create some games and situations to help your child preserve his own creative urges. There isn't any penalty for being a creative parent.

Saying Yes to Creativity

 I do realize that this chapter is based on what might be a controversial assumption—that being creative is a desired virtue for both children and adults who would still like to be children. It might seem that the adult world demands and rewards conformity—that creativity gets in the way of production and success; but I don't agree.

 None of us know what God has in store for our children. But I do know that we should do whatever we can to prepare them to be happy in the circumstances in which they find themselves.

 I am convinced that a creative person, a truly creative person, spends fewer hours of his life being bored or grumpy. He may not be any richer or more successful or more powerful, but he should be a little more excited about living.

 A classic story illustrates this point. A reporter went out to check on the construction of a new church. One craftsman was skillfully sanding beautiful wooden beams for the ceiling. When the reporter asked what he was doing, he gruffly replied, "I am sanding a beam. What does it look like?"

 Next, the reporter spoke with the craftsman assembling magnificent stained-glass windows. Again, the answer was terse. "I am making a stained-glass window. What does it look like?"

 Finally, the reporter stopped the man who had been given the task of sweeping up behind the two skilled craftsmen. "What are you doing?" the reporter asked.

"I am building a temple for the worship of God," the sweeper proclaimed.

I want my child to be the kind of person who builds temples rather than sands beams. I want him to have an imagination big enough to see the truth.

Homework Assignments for Parents

1. To what extent do you want your child to be creative? When do you want him to conform? Is he aware of what you expect from him at these different times?

2. What are some new creative games or experiences you can participate in with your child this week?

3. In what ways can you help increase your child's imagination?

16

The Changing Role of Television

ne commonly discussed area where you can help your child develop responsibility is that of television viewing. It would be easy for me to go into a long tirade here, warning you about that demon monster we have allowed into our houses. I could tell you about the research which shows that children learn aggressiveness and even violence from TV. I could talk about the absurd programming which brings into our family rooms sights and suggestions that weren't fit fare for an adult twenty years ago. Or I could simply relate the information that the average American school child spends about six hours per day in front of the TV—one-fourth of his life.

But I am going to resist the urge to remind you of these things, because television is a reality. Whether or not we like the box or the programming, we are still living in a television society.

Your child will live all his life in the company of TV. We really don't solve any problems by denying the existence of television; we only postpone them.

The Up Side of TV

Television is here to stay, and it has the potential of being an effective teaching instrument in our society. The concept of television is actually a good learning idea. In most learning situations, we employ only one sense. We either hear something or we see something. In television, we see and hear at the same time, so the potential for our learning is vastly increased—more than doubled. But this fact makes the programming even more significant.

Since television is such an effective teaching tool, we need to be cautious about what we allow ourselves and our children to learn from it. We need to learn how to use television, and we need to teach our children how to use it. Unfortunately not enough of us have mastered that lesson yet.

The appropriate time to begin that study, if you have not already, is when the child begins his journey into school and reading. Both these intellectual and social activities heighten his awareness. As his vocabulary and attention span develop, he will simply receive more stimuli from a television program. He will hear more words, see more scenes, and respond to more situations.

As he develops the ability to organize, he will retain more of what he has seen. As he learns to interact with what he is reading, his emotional response to television will increase. In simple terms, watching TV is a different activity for a reader than for a nonreader. If you have a TV in your home, you need to be aware of this transition because your child is going to need some instruction and supervision.

Problem #1: The Intense Impact of Real Life

For one thing, your child will soon be able to distinguish between reality and fantasy. At that time, he will need some help in dealing with emotions during programs that are most realistic. He may be able to recognize the bloody, unreal detective shows as so much imagination, which can be passed off easily. But a program such as "Little House on the Prairie" may make a deep impression.

Since television is such a powerful tool, his emotions during such real-life drama could become quite intense. If he watches such drama, you will have to watch with him. You will need to offer him counsel and encouragement.

Let me illustrate. One Saturday afternoon, my wife and I watched an old Western movie. In the space of two hours we saw about fourteen guys get blown away in some kind of violence or another. At the end of the movie, we watched about fifteen minutes of a live sports program. A high diver hit the water incorrectly and lay at the bottom of the pool until the rescuers could pull him up. We were almost in a state of shock as we sat glued to our seats, watching this drama unfold before our eyes.

We had just watched fourteen guys get blown away in fictional death, but the possibility of real death disturbed us greatly. Because the scene was too personal and demanded too much emotion, I almost wished I weren't watching; yet I couldn't bring myself to the point of actually turning off the set. Through this medium of television, I was trapped. I found comfort in having my wife present so we could talk about the event as it happened, and we discussed it occasionally in the weeks that followed. Obviously, both of us still remember it. The picture was too real for us to forget the moment.

Television has the power of bringing that same kind of experience to your child. How he needs someone with him when that moment comes! Study carefully what you let him watch by himself. Not only does he need you to help him through the moral problems some programs present, but he may need you to help him manage the emotional problems that arise out of the programs which are closer to his reality.

Problem #2: TV's Effect on Concentration

Another problem that comes from a constant diet of television watching is that it teaches the child to turn outside stimuli—visual and aural—off and on at will. This ability isn't much of an asset when a teacher is trying to tell the class the events leading to the Revolutionary War. But it's not hard to understand how the child develops the habit. Living in a room with a constant flow of pictures and sounds—some interesting and some not so interesting—can really foul up our ability to concentrate.

The solution to this problem may be rather simple: Turn the set off occasionally. I am not opposed to letting children watch a given program. In fact, a good television program will frequently inspire a child to read, to think, or even to create. But we cannot allow TV to become an opium which lulls us into states of semi-consciousness.

To control this situation, use the on-and-off switch. If there is a program you and your child want to watch, watch it. But when it is over, turn the set off. Fill the room with silence and imagination. Eliminate that thing which is demanding semiattention so that you can concentrate fully on the reality at hand.

Actually, this idea isn't original with me. I learned it in a teaching book which warned me about leaving the overhead projector on after it had served its usefulness to the class. We can just receive so many stimuli at a given time. If we get too many, we lose our ability to concentrate. Any generation raised on a television diet is susceptible to this malady.

Problem #3: Reduction of Creativity and Mental Discipline

Television also permits the child to be passive mentally. Why do we need to draw mental images when someone will draw them for us? But drawing mental images is basic to our intellect. Between the ages of six and eight, the child learns to create, formulate, and plan through the exercise of drawing mental pictures, either from what he is reading or from what he makes up himself. If he begins to rely too heavily on television, he could lose the thrill of making his own pictures.

You can prevent this by making sure your child has ample opportunity to read and to imagine. You may want to use his favorite TV show as a starting point. Have him write the next show. If he can't write yet, let him dictate the show to you and you write it for him. Have him put the characters in unusual places, meeting unusual people. Activate your child in language activities. Make sure he is speaking, writing, and reading. Too much absorbing will only make him intellectually, and perhaps physically, flabby.

Problem #4: Tendency to Reduce Exercise Time

This leads us to the next point. Between the ages of six and eight, your child will grow intellectually and spiritually, but he is also growing physically. During this time he needs lots of exercise. What he gets at school is simply not enough. Of course, if your child is active and creative, you may get the idea that he gets too much exercise; but if he is a passive child, he could rely on the television as an excuse for not getting the exercise his developing body needs.

Just turning off the set may not be sufficient in this case. You may have to learn to play yourself, or you may need to introduce him to activities outside the home and school.

We can say a lot of negative things about the use and abuse of television. Very probably, the problems will never resolve themselves. It's up to parents to take the initiative and make sure that television remains a positive influence on the family.

Your child will watch you to see what your attitudes are toward television. And what could you ever expect to watch on the TV screen that could compare to watching your child grow up into a healthy, informed person?

Homework Assignments for Parents

1. Have you identified problems with TV use in your home? If so, what are you doing about them?

2. In what ways could you use TV to reinforce other topics already discussed in this book—reading, writing, math, creativity, etc.?

3. What are some realistic ways you can reduce the amount of time your child watches TV alone?

17

Love and Approval

Ginger is a cheerful second grader with long blonde doggie ears. I really enjoy her company because she loves life. When we are together, we spend much of our time playing math games. She is really good with numbers, so it is hard to trick her. And she is always eager to learn something new, so I usually spend some time preparing for the next time we get together.

The other day, Ginger looked over my shoulder as I wrote our names to record our scores of the game we were playing. She wanted to see how I made my loops and controlled the pen. Because of her high interest in my writing, we took the opportunity to practice some preliminary steps to cursive writing—"preteaching," the experts call it.

I was pleased to see Ginger's curiosity and her eagerness to move further ahead into an unknown world. I asked her if she would get to learn cursive during second grade. In recent years, this has become standard fare for some second graders.

"No," she said, rather forlornly. "Only the smart kids get to learn cursive in the second grade."

I knew immediately what she meant. In her classroom, students are placed into groups according to reading abilities. Since Ginger doesn't read as well as some of the other students, she is in one of the average reading groups.

It's easy to defend this as an educational practice. Students are placed in groups with people who all work at about the same speed. A teacher can choose different books for different groups, and the teachers can tackle specific problems. It probably makes sense that the more advanced groups will get to try new things before the end of second grade. The students need the enticement, the carrot on the end of the stick. Besides, we can assume that those advanced students are more mature physically than the others, so they should be able to handle the dexterity that cursive writing requires.

But try explaining all that to Ginger. All she knows about educational theory is that some kids get to try something new and inviting while she and her other colleagues have their curiosities stuck in the same old stuff. I am not sure it makes sense to her.

One of the toughest jobs of parenthood may be explaining to the Gingers who live at our houses why the system works this way. But the challenge doesn't stop there. We must learn to explain these things to her in such a way that her plaintive cry, "The smart kids get to do it," doesn't become the motto of her life. How do we prevent her from convincing herself that she is, in fact, second rate?

Common-sense Love

I know you love your child. You have loved him ever since he was born, and yours is a constant love. Regardless of what he does or becomes, your love will stay unchanged. This is something he can always count on. Yet when your child starts school, both of you will encounter some circumstances that will give you new opportunities to express that love in practical terms.

For one thing, you will find that you need to develop a responsive kind of love so you can react to situations rather than creating them. When your child is at home with you all day, *you* create learning situations and control the variables. But at school, your child will encounter social situations and learning situations that are outside your control. You can share vicariously with what your child is going through, but you simply don't have the same emotional involvement as you would if you had created the situation.

When your child first wanders away from the nest and treks off to school, there are a whole bundle of setbacks and frustrations waiting to snare him. He isn't learning something as quickly as his classmates. He lost the race at recess. The class bully is pushing him around. His artwork was not selected for the bulletin board. His crayon broke. The teacher yelled at him for running to the window to watch the fire truck. Two other kids always sit in the same seat on the bus and won't let him in. In the P.E. bombardment game, he was the last one chosen. Some kids teased him when he got glasses, or braces, or a black eye.

With all the trouble in the Mideast, these may not sound like major problems. But when a person is only seven years old and his world doesn't even include a Mideast, these are real frustrations. The people who would help him through these trying times need to understand the significance of such problems. They are real and they need attention. How you respond to these real problems depends largely on what kind of person you are and what kind of person your child is. Let's look at three possibilities: diversion, direct instruction, and consistency.

Diversion

If the child is suffering some setbacks at school, help get his mind off these problems by creating some successful learning experiences outside school. Have him wash the car. Teach him to ride a bike without training wheels. Open a savings account. Take him to a movie.

It could be that school has introduced him to the first real setback he has ever experienced, and this could be devastating to his confidence. But when you establish diversionary situations where he can succeed, he may regain enough confidence to work out his own frustrations at school.

Direct Instruction

As your child encounters new conflict experiences, such as bullies or rude children (or even rude adults), you may want to give him specific directions on how to manage relationships with those people. If you decide to go this route, make sure your directions are workable. Too often we give instructions that are easier to give than to follow.

If you sense that your child is frightened of the class bully, try not to tell him to punch the guy in the nose. Regardless of what you think of the role of violence in human relationships, that is poor advice. (Would you punch Mr. T in the nose?) If you choose to give instructions to help your child handle setbacks, you need to be very specific. Make sure he understands how he can implement the information you have provided. If you give directions from Scripture, make sure he sees the practical application.

Consistency

Regardless of the kinds of problems your child brings home from school and regardless of the kinds of problems he creates himself, maintain a constant, consistent, loving environment. He needs the experience of being comfortable and accepted for at least part of his day. This consistency and acceptance will provide him with the opportunity to refuel his confidence and identity so he can face the more unpleasant situations.

During the period when your child is adjusting to school life, he may actually create an unusual trap for himself. When school first starts, he will probably discover a new wave of independence. He may even choose to flaunt his freedom a bit. Now that he has friends and a life of his own, he simply doesn't need family support as much as he once did.

He may try to draw away by building some fences to show you that he is growing. But when the trials, frustrations, setbacks, and failures come, he may want to find solace by returning to a simpler, safer time. That is a fairly normal reaction. When the present gets me down, I find comfort in remembering the safety of the past.

But if your child has already built the fences, he may not know how to get back to a time when it was all right to sit on your lap and receive your hugs. Since he now has the power to read on his own, he may not know how to return to a time when you read the bedtime story and tucked him in. This is why I recommend consistency. Regardless of how independent he tries to become, make sure you are giving enough cues so he knows he is still welcome to retreat to your lap and regroup.

Keeping Things in Perspective

One of my young friends started kindergarten last year. Since he and I are pals, we have had frequent conversations about such things as sports, movies, ice-cream trucks, books, and God. I find him a stimulating conversationalist. He is polite, and he is confident enough to be at ease around adults. After his third day in school, he came trudging home with a note attached to his shirt:

Dear Mr. and Mrs. X:

*Because of his disregard and
disinterest for school and classroom
policy, George's behavior has become
a matter of immediate concern.
Please call and make an appointment
to meet with me.*

Sincerely,

Mrs. Kindergarten Teacher

I think I know why parents are often frightened of their children's teachers. I would be trembling, too, if I had to meet the lady who sent this note. But after I got the parents quieted down and reassured of some self-dignity, I persuaded them to muster the courage to go see her.

It seems that George did not know how to write his name as well as the other children, so he turned in his papers without a name. Personally, I thought it was a rather intelligent solution to the problem, but turning in a paper without a name is an absolute no-no in the academic world. I think the teacher was also disturbed because George didn't show any noticeable remorse over his inability to perform. He had simply not learned the right attitude toward his weakness.

I am probably coming down too hard on this teacher, but she illustrates an important point. Teachers, by the very nature of their assignments, tend to see immediate actions and results. All the influence that a specific teacher will ever have in the life of your child must be packed into nine months. She has to see the results of her work in that same limited school year. Sometimes this short-term focus intensifies the teacher's response to growth or lack of growth in a specific area.

George was all right. He is capable, active, and happy. If nothing more traumatic than this happens to him, he is going to have a full childhood and a solid life.

So this is your challenge as you help your child get acclimated to school and school activities: *You need to respond to the joys and frustrations of the moment, but you also need to keep your responses in the perspective of a total life.*

A child's primary career is, at best, only a fleeting moment in the space of a lifetime. There is so much packed into such a few weeks, so many new beginnings. Between the ages of six and eight, your child will start to school for the first and only time in his life. He will learn to read for the first and only time. He will have first-, second-, and third-grade teachers for the first and only time. He will memorize his arithmetic facts, write his name, and perform a variety of new skills and acquire a variety of new attitudes.

As he grows past this stage of life and enters other eras, let's pray that he leaves with more than mere skills and attitudes. Let's pray that during that time of "first and only" he has picked up some events, some significant moments which constitute the stuff of memories, happy memories resting at the threshold of his mind—moments to be called back into the memory to fill those empty mental spaces as he waits at a red light or just before he drops off to sleep at night, or when he helps your grandchild learn to count past twenty.

My wise professor used to say, "Having a child is taking out a twenty-year mortgage on your emotions, energy, time, and money." As my children were growing, I decided he knew what he was talking about. Now that my children are grown, I have decided that the mortgage is even longer than he said.

Throughout this book, I have focused discussion on helping children at a very special age—the age between six and eight, when they first discover the world beyond home and parents. In asking for your understanding, I have described some emotional, physical, and educational situations which people this age usually encounter, and I have made suggestions which I hope will help you help your child during this time of adjustment. But the most significant piece of advice I have to give is the counsel of my professor: *remember the length of the mortgage.*

As you help your child master the skill required to function in his changing world, you can also help him drive the pegs on which to hang those memories. Soon, too soon, his primary years will be over, only to live in memory. But if the two of you experience those years together, you will always hold the memories together. And that is the bond of parenthood.

Homework Assignments for Parents

1. What school experiences is your child facing for which he needs your support? How can you let him know you understand what he's going through?

2. What new experiences can you undertake with your child to help him forget school traumas? Make a mental list so you'll be ready for the next "emergency."

3. If and when a teacher becomes concerned about your child's behavior, do you try to look past the teacher's perspective to see the situation as your child does? If so, how can you then mediate between child and teacher?

4. In what ways are you preparing to cope with the emotional "mortgage" you will encounter during the next several years?